Pas ...iis Test

Second edition

10-2008

TES

Consciencious
Synopsis
Atrocious
accommodate

Passing the Literacy Skills Test

Second edition

Jim Johnson

LearningMatters

Acknowledgements

The publishers would like to thank the TDA for permission to use the audio icon on page 2. This has been taken from the practice Literacy Skills Test on the TDA website www.tda. gov.uk and is the copyright of the Training and Development Agency.

First published in 2001 by Learning Matters Ltd
Reprinted in 2001, 2002, 2003 (twice), 2004, 2005 (twice), 2006 and 2007 (twice).
Second edition published in 2008.

British Library Cataloguing in Publication Data
A CIP record for this book is available from the British Library.

ISBN 978 1 84445 167 8

Cover design by Topics – The Creative Partnership
Text design by Code 5 Design Associates Ltd
Project Management by Deer Park Productions, Tavistock
Typeset by PDQ Typesetting Ltd, Newcastle under Lyme
Printed and bound in Great Britain by Cromwell Press, Trowbridge, Wiltshire

Learning Matters Ltd
33 Southernhay East
Exeter EX1 1NX
Tel: 01392 215560
info@learningmatters.co.uk
www.learningmatters.co.uk

Contents

Series introduction

The QTS Skills Test

From 1 September 2008, all new trainee teachers will only be awarded QTS status if they successfully pass the skills tests. This removes the 'five-year grace period', which previously enabled trainees to practise as unqualified teachers without completing the skills tests for up to five years. All new entrants into the teaching profession in England will now have to pass the skills tests to be eligible for the award of QTS, including those on School Centred Initial Teacher Training and Graduate and Registered Teacher Programmes (GRTP).

The three tests cover skills in:

- **numeracy;**
- **literacy;**
- **information and communication technology (ICT).**

The tests will demonstrate that you can apply these skills to the degree necessary for their use in your day-to-day work in a school, rather than the subject knowledge required for teaching. The tests are taken online by booking a time at a specified centre, are marked instantly and your result, along with feedback on that result, will be given to you before you leave the centre.

You can find more information about the skills tests and the specified centres on the Training and Development Agency for Schools (TDA) website: www.tda.gov.uk.

Titles in this series

This series of books is designed to help you become familiar with the skills you will need to pass the tests and to practise questions on each of the topic areas to be tested.

Passing the Numeracy Skills Test (fourth edition)
Mark Patmore
ISBN 978 1 84445 169 2

Passing the Literacy Skills Test (second edition)
Jim Johnson
ISBN 978 1 84445 167 8

Passing the ICT Skills Test (third edition)
Clive Ferrigan
ISBN 978 1 84445 168 5

To order, please contact our distributors:
BEBC Distribution, Albion Close, Parkstone, Poole BH12 3LL
Tel: 0845 230 9000 Email: learningmatters@bebc.co.uk

Introduction

As a student-teacher, you have to pass a test of your own literacy if you are to be granted QTS. This applies to all teachers, whether they see themselves as having an English specialism or not. This book is designed to help you to pass that test. The necessary knowledge is explained, examples of questions are provided and answers to those questions are supplied, along with *Key Points* to indicate the main things that need attention.

The areas covered in the book – spelling, punctuation, comprehension and grammar – are the ones that appear in the test. The particular aspects of spelling, etc., are also the ones that are in the test. The actual form of the questions is also similar. Everything you will be tested on is explained; examples are given and the questions give you plenty of practice for the test. The questions in the test will be a selection from the types of question shown here in each section.

Why is student-teachers' knowledge of English being tested?

Teachers need to have a confident knowledge of English. A (student-)teacher who has a sound idea of how the English language is organised can help children to use it well. Some of the teaching approaches promoted by the Primary National Strategy – especially guided writing – can only be successful if the teacher knows, for example, what it is about a piece of writing by a child that makes it good and also knows how it could be improved.

Teachers receive a great deal of written information and have to be able to understand it and act on it with assurance. They often have to write, or collaborate in writing, documents such as school policies, reports on their children, information for parents, etc.

Finally, teachers and their use of English are very much in the public eye. Parents, governors, inspectors and others see them in their professional role and, inevitably, make judgements. Teachers need to know enough and be competent enough to deal confidently with the world they move in.

Above all, the right of children to be taught by somebody who knows enough about English to be able to help them is the basis of the test and of this book.

What is the test like?

The test will be carried out online. For the spelling test, you will also use headphones.

You will be asked:

- **to type in your answers for Spelling and Punctuation;**
- **in Grammar, to drag to a specified line whichever you think is the best answer out of several multiple-choice options;**
- **and, in Comprehension, to drag a tick symbol, an acronym (such as QTS) or an ordinal number (such as THIRD) into a box by the best of several possible answers.**

You will not be tested on the National Curriculum nor on how to teach English. You will be tested on four main sections of knowledge about literacy: spelling, punctuation, comprehension and grammar.

The spelling section of the test *has* to be attempted first. Once the spelling section is done, you must go on to the other sections and cannot return to spelling. There is no restriction on how you go about the other three sections: do them in any order, tackle questions within each section in any order and move about among those three sections as much as you like. It may make more sense to do the grammar test last but that is up to you.

The pass mark for each of the three skills tests is 60%. Spelling has a total of 10 marks, Punctuation 15, Comprehension 8–12 and Grammar 8–12. If, as is likely, the test has 48 questions, 29 correct answers can gain you a pass.

This is what the four sections cover and how they are approached in the test:

Spelling

Teachers are expected to spell correctly. That includes the sorts of words that are likely to appear in their professional work. The emphasis on correct spelling is justified because correct spelling is easier to read than bad spelling. In the test, you are expected to use British English spelling but either *-ize* or *-ise* verb-endings will be allowed.

You will need to wear headphones for this part of the test. You will see a group of sentences on the computer screen that have had some words deleted. Where a word has been deleted, there appears an icon for *Audio* 🔊. When you reach that word in your reading, click the icon and listen through your headphones. You will hear the deleted word. Decide how you think it is spelled and type your decision directly into the box provided in the deletion space. If you need to hear a word more than once, there is no problem. You may also make several attempts to spell a word but you should keep in mind that the whole test allows only about 45 minutes.

If you have trouble with hearing, a silent, multiple-choice alternative will be made available for you.

As this is a book, not a computer, the practice questions are multiple choice. This is the sort of question you are likely to meet in the book:

In the following passage, you are shown four alternative spellings for some words. Read the passage and then underline the alternative that you believe is correct:

Once we have seen all the reciepts/receits/receipts/reciets for this term, we can make a more professionnal/profesional/proffesional/professional judgement about our financial planning.

Punctuation

Teachers are expected to be able to read and use punctuation correctly, especially those texts that they are likely to encounter or to produce as part of their professional work. Punctuation that is consistent and that follows the conventions makes a text easy to read. Errors in punctuation not only give a reader more work to do but also leave a bad impression that is not made better if the error was caused by carelessness. Knowing what punctuation is needed and where it should go reveal both an awareness of the reader's needs and, fundamentally, a high degree of literacy.

Unlike spelling, there is a personal element in punctuation. By the time you have finished the book, you might have noticed that I use more semicolons than most people. Many writers never use semicolons at all. The point is that, if they are used, they should be used consistently.

The point about consistency is such a key one that it is worth considering it here. Suppose you have written this sentence:

My early experience with the class has led me to modify my medium-term plans.

Now suppose that you want to add something to that sentence to express, however mildly, your feelings about having to make the changes. You decide to add the word *unfortunately*. That word can go at the beginning of the sentence (with a comma immediately after it) or at the end (with a comma immediately before it) or in the middle, between *me* and *to*. That is an interruption in the grammatical structure of the sentence and such interruptions are marked by commas. A common failing is to put just one comma, either before or after the interruption, but you actually need two; like this:

My early experience with the class has led me, unfortunately, to modify my medium-term plans.

Consistency means that you do not put just one comma in this case but that you use both. They are partners.

The test is presented online. You will see a text or texts that have some punctuation but not all that they need. Your task is to identify where in the texts you should place a punctuation mark, change a lower case letter for an upper case one or make a new paragraph. When you have decided what change to make, double click on the word you have chosen to edit – the word before the punctuation mark – and a dialogue box will appear. The word you clicked will appear in a box. Type in your punctuation and click OK. The box will disappear and the word and your punctuation choice will appear in the text but will now be blue. To add a new paragraph, double click on the word before the new paragraph is to begin, click on the letter 'P' which is in the dialogue box and click OK. You can change your answer if you think you should.

Sometimes, although it is possible to insert a punctuation mark, it may not be necessary or even appropriate. You have to decide. What is very important is that you add marks, etc., so that you create a text whose punctuation is wholly consistent. Your criterion is to ask yourself what would be *consistent with the existing punctuation*.

This is the sort of question you are likely to meet in the book. As this is a book, not a computer, you cannot type in your chosen punctuation mark; instead, you simply note which punctuation mark or other change in punctuation is necessary at which point to make the whole consistent. There will be passages like this for you to practise your knowledge of punctuation; your job is to make it appropriate and consistent in its use of punctuation:

although the literacy framework had been working well some staff wondered how to maintain the good work they had done in other areas of the curriculum could drama and pe be retained at the same level as previously

Grammar

Teachers need to be able to see whether a piece of writing is, or is not, in standard English, the variety of English that is required in formal texts and, therefore, in almost all writing. They also need to be able to say if the text makes sense and, if not, what prevents it from making sense. Finally, they need to be aware of the style that is appropriate to a particular type of text and to understand what, if anything, is wrong with the style.

The test is multiple-choice. You will see a passage that is not quite complete; bits of language are missing. The decision about what should be inserted to complete the passage is a grammatical choice. You will be shown a range of possible bits of language to insert, only one of which would complete that part of the passage satisfactorily. The choice of that insertion will depend on your reading the whole passage carefully as well as the sentence that has to be completed. You insert your choice simply by dragging it into position.

Below is an example of a sentence that is incomplete. Four possible ways of completing the sentence are offered. Your task is to choose the one that fits grammatically:

The assembly was concerned with the series of playground incidents

Now choose one of the following to complete the sentence:

(a) *that were making life difficult for the infants.*
(b) *that was making life difficult for the infants.*
(c) *that are making life difficult for the infants.*
(d) *that is making life difficult for the infants.*

Comprehension

Teachers receive a good deal of written material that they must understand and make some response to. This puts an emphasis on close, analytical reading. You will need to read with attention to the main ideas, with an awareness of its argument and, sometimes, with an idea of how it affects your existing ideas. You might need to make judgements about the text and to organise and reorganise its content. Since that is what being a teacher now involves, the test assesses your ability to read in this way.

The test is multiple-choice. You will be asked to decide which of several possible answers is the best or correct one and to drag a tick symbol ✓, a word or an acronym into a box next to your chosen answer.

The test will present you with the sorts of text that teachers are likely to see and read as part of their professional lives. You will be expected to identify key points, read between the lines, tell fact from fiction, make judgements, etc. Not every test will examine every aspect!

At its simplest, the test might ask you to identify the meaning of words and phrases. Remember that no one test will test every aspect of every one of the four sections. In the following short passage, for example, you are asked to say who you think is the intended audience for the text:

You will have seen from the local press, where results are published from every school in the Authority, that this school has had a consistently high standard of performance in the annual SATs over several years. This fine record is expected to continue for some years, at least. A consequence of this success is that the school is oversubscribed each year and, regretfully, it is not always possible to offer a place to every child whose parents apply to us.

How to prepare for the test

- **Use this book to get a good grasp of what understanding is demanded by the test.**
- **Go to the TDA website (www.tda.gov.uk/skillstests/literacy.aspx) to read their advice, familiarise yourself with the test and what it looks like and try the practice tests.**
- **From that practice, identify what you need to brush up and refer to this book.**
- **Remember that doing well in spelling and punctuation can take you close to the pass mark.**
- **Read again the Hints in each section of this book.**

How the book is organised

For the purposes of the test, literacy is seen as comprising the four sections detailed above: spelling, punctuation, grammar and comprehension. Each section has its own chapter. There you will find an explanation of the knowledge required, examples of the features of literacy being tested and explicit direction about what to do in the test. There are practice questions for each section.

There are answers to the practice questions in each chapter. Each answer is explained and the key points that you need to attend to are pointed out. There is a list of suggested reading and a Glossary.

1 | Spelling

Introduction

10 marks are available for spelling.

If you want to write well, good spelling is not as important as good grammar or even good punctuation but it is still important. Some great writers have been poor spellers; some bad writers can spell any word they need.

Correct spelling is not a mark of intelligence but it is very helpful to a reader because poor spelling interferes with the flow of easy reading. If a text is correctly written, the good spellings will not be noticed because all the reader's attention has gone straight to the meaning. Ideally, when someone reads what you write, they should be able to pay attention to what you want to say, to your meaning, and not be distracted by poor spelling. Bad spelling interferes with the reader's attention just as a fault in glass can interfere with the view through a window.

There are no tricks in the test; you will not have to learn how to spell *phthisis* especially for the occasion. If you can spell the kinds of word that are in common use, especially in the world of education, you will have no problems. British spelling rather than American is expected although either *-ise* or *-ize* at the ends of some verbs is acceptable. However, be consistent in your use of whichever you choose.

The actual form of the test is described in the Introduction. For this practice test, you will be given short passages with four optional spellings for you to choose from for each 'problem word'.

Essential knowledge

The commonest spelling problem for adults, even educated and well-read adults, is when to use a **double consonant**, as in:

accommodation	*exaggerate*	*harass*
committee	*success*	*assess*
professional	*apprentice*	*misspell*

Unfortunately, there is no easy way to remember them. They have to be learned by heart. What does help is simply to write a good deal. If you are in the habit of writing, even brief notes to yourself to help you to think through an issue, all aspects of your writing (with the probable exception of handwriting!) will improve. As with so much in life, use it or lose it.

It does help you if you notice those words that you know give you trouble. Look at the following list of some double-consonant words and copy out any that you suspect have been problems for you in the past. When you have a list, look at each in turn, remember the *whole word,* its sequences of letters, its prefix and suffix (if any), and try to write it again. Then check it.

abbreviate	(in)efficient
acclimatise	immeasurable
allowed	miscellaneous
apparent	miscellany
appear	occur/occurred
apprentice	occurrence
approach	omit/omission
appropriate	opportunity
approve	parallel
approximate	passage
assess	permissible
challenge	permission
commensurate	possess
commit/committed	proceed (but precede)
correspondence	questionnaire
correspondent	recommend
curriculum	recur/recurrence
disappear	satellite
dissipate	succeed
embarrass	success
excellent	succinct
grammar	terrible
grip/gripped	truthfully
happily	till (but until)
harass	vacillate

There is a special category of words with double consonants. Some stem words, like *fulfil* in *fulfilling*, end in a single consonant – that is, a vowel and a consonant – but then double the final consonant if either *-ed* or *-ing* is added. Some other words in this category are:

commit   *begin*

Note: Benefit, benefited *are exceptions.*

Remarkably, since spelling is normally either right or wrong, you are allowed two choices for *bias* and *focus*. Both *biassed* and *biased* and *focussed* and *focused* are acceptable spellings.

> **HINT** Some spellings just have to be learned. Make a list of your own 'hard words'.

We spell words in English in the way we do for a variety of reasons, such as trying to represent:

- **a difference in meaning, despite a similarity in sound – for example, *there, their, they're*;**
- **related meanings, despite some variation in sound – for example, *medicine, medical, medicinal*;**
- **an earlier pronunciation – for example, *knight*;**
- **a foreign origin – for example, *chalet*.**

If the way we sound words was the only guide to their spelling, *phonics* might be spelled *fonnix*. But the main reason for spelling words as we do is that they **represent the sounds we speak**. This often seems unlikely but it does account for more spelling features than any other factor. Therefore, it helps to use this when learning some words that are fairly regular phonically.

Some of the words that can be learned like this are:

homophone   *pronounce*   *pronunciation*   *effect*

It can help to see if a word you find hard to spell can be pronounced in a way that reminds you of its spelling. On the other hand, be careful. Some words have the same sound – in the following examples, *e* – but are written differently:

ate   *jeopardy*   *pleasure*   *said*

A few words are often pronounced wrongly. *Mischievous* is sometimes spoken with an *ee* sound before the *-ous* and the speller needs to beware of that influence.

Although the sound/letter correspondence is so important in English, it still needs to be recognised that there are many **homophones**: words that sound alike but do not look alike or mean the same thing.

Learn by heart words that cannot be learned in any other way. One other way, in some cases, might be to invent a mnemonic. The student who wrote:

The children took too my personality.

might have been helped by something like:

Two *days ago, I went* **to** *work despite feeling* **too** *tired to get up.*

Other homophones include:

allot/a lot	*meet/meat*
aloud/allowed	*pare/pear*
ate/eight	*practise/practice*
doe/dough	*read/red*
due/dew	*sore/saw*
hare/hair	*wait/weight*
lead/led	*wear/where*
lent/leant	*wheel/weal*

Incidentally, although students have asked me on three occasions to 'explain the difference between *as* with an *h* and *as* without an *h*', this is not strictly a homophone. It is simply a reminder that the way in which any of us speaks is not always a good guide to how words are written.

Some words seem to be easily confused. Students have written:

people off all ages

instead of:

people of all ages.

Some write:

could of

instead of:

could have.

The difference is in meaning in the case of *off* instead of *of* and in grammar in the case of *of* instead of *have*. *Off* is used to mean something like *movement from a position,* as in *jump off, take off, off with his head.* After a modal verb such as *could,* you need another, main, verb such as *have,* not a preposition like *of.*

Some words are best learned by heart, such as those that either look as if, by analogy, they should be spelled like another word you know or those that simply have no analogy. These include such words as:

awe	*merit*	*schedule*
awful	*mileage*	*scheme*
curiosity	*monotonous*	*separate*
curious	*naive*	*sixth*
eighth	*occasion*	*suspicion*
fifth	*prestige*	*table*
half	*prevail*	*thorough*
halves	*prevalent*	*tried*
heroes	*psychiatrist*	*try*
humour	*pursue*	*twelfth*
humorous	*repertoire*	*unanimous*
ideology	*queue*	*vicious*
judgement	*rhyme*	
label	*rhythm*	
ladle	*sceptic*	

Notice that some words have a pattern of letters that is fairly consistent – for example, the four-vowel pattern of a repeated *ue* in *queue,* the *-ous* endings in *humorous.* Some words, like *prevail* and *prevalent,* not only add a morpheme (such as *-ent*) when they become another part of speech but also change the spelling of the stem-word (the *i* is dropped from *prevail* as the *u* is dropped from *humour* when it is changed to *humorous*).

Some words are spelled one way when they are nouns and another way when they are verbs:

Noun: *practice   advice*   Verb: *practise   advise*

If you could say *the* before a word, it is a noun and ends in *-ice*. If you could say *I, you, we, they* before it, it is a verb and ends in *-ise*.

Some long words can be broken down into parts:

   miscellany = *misc + ell + any*

You need to notice the features of each part: the *sc;* the double *ll;* the recognisable word *any*.

Some words can be broken down into smaller words:

   weather = w + eat + her   *together = to + get + her*

I confess my indebtedness to a boy aged five for revealing that truth about *together*!

Remember the patterns – the sequences of letters – in words that repeat particular letters:

   minimise   curriculum   remember

Remember is often misspelled, simply because of the crowded repetition of *e* and *m*.

Notice what happens when a **suffix** is added.

Just as *humour* loses its second *u* when it becomes *humorous,* so we find other changes when a word takes a suffix:

To form the plural of a word that ends in *y,* drop the *y* and add *ies*:

   fairy   fairies   country   countries

To add *-ed* or *-ing* to a verb that ends in *-e,* drop the e:

   manage   managed   managing
   create   created   creating
   solve   solved   solving

If you can develop a feel for the ways that English words are built, for their **morphology**, it will help you to see where one part ends and another begins. This can help particularly with longer and less common words and with the common affixes:

   mis + take   dis + tinc + tion   dis + agree + able

It is not obvious but the suffix is *-tion*, not *-ion*.

HINT	Note that the prefixes *mis* and *dis* end in one *s* only. That helps when you add *dis* to *appear* to make *disappear*: not *dissappear*.

Some words, connected by meaning – and in these cases, therefore, by spelling – vary a little in the way they sound but that has to be ignored:

photo   photograph   photographer   photographic

The letters *sc* represent the *s* sound if the following letter is *e* or *i*:

discipline   adolescent   descent

On the other hand, they represent the *sk* sound if the following letter is *r, l, a, o, u*:

discrepancy   discussion

When do you write *ie* and when do you write *ei*? This rule works:

For the sound *ee,* put *ie* as in:

believe   mischief   niece

For the sound *ee,* put *e* before *i* when the preceding letter is *c*:

conceive   deceive   receive

However, this only applies to words where the sound is *ee* and not to words like:

weight   forfeit   friend

Many people ignore that last part of the rule.

HINT   *i* before *e*, except after *c, when the sound is ee.*

Most words that end with the sound in *recent* use *-ent*:

confident	*emergent*	*equivalent*	*excellent*
impatient	*independent*	*prevalent*	*reminiscent*

Very few words use *-ant*:

preponderant	*quadrant*	*redundant*

HINT   Since far more words end in *-ent* or *-ence*, it pays to focus on and learn any that end in *-ant* or *-ance.*

A very common error is to use the wrong letters to represent the vowel sound in *sir*. Words like these just have to be learned by heart:

*pur*sue   sep**a**rate   b**ir**d   w**or**d

The sound *s* is often written with a *c,* especially if the *c* is followed by an *e* or *i,* as in:

concede   deficit   necessary

Sometimes, it is written with a -ce, especially at the end of a word:

practice   *prejudice*

Sometimes, it is written with an *s*, even when it is not expected:

idiosyncrasy   *consensus*   *supersede*

Or with an -se:

practise   *premise*

And even with -sc:

miscellaneous   *miscellany*   *scene*

General tips

Keep a dictionary nearby to check problem words and then try to learn them. Look out for commonly used letter-strings, for affixes and other morphological features and simply for anything unusual.

See if you tend to make similar errors, such as not noticing that *separate* has an *a* in the middle or that *develop*, unlike *envelope*, does not end with an *e*.

Try sounding out. On the whole, words that are phonically regular do not cause spelling problems but some writers lose their faith in that regularity. Try it.

Look at the whole of a word, not just its letters, and try to remember that whole. If it helps, say the letters to yourself rhythmically.

Look for possible analogies; for example, *eight*, *height* and *weight*.

Pay special attention to the letter-strings in foreign words. Their foreignness includes their combining letters quite differently from English.

Do not trust the spell check on a word processor. Any spell check will allow *top* when you meant *to*, *were* when you meant *where* and *feather* when you meant *father*. A spell check will correct non-words, like *teh* when the writer intended *the*, but it is still necessary to read through a late draft to check the spelling yourself.

If you know which words you tend to get wrong when you use a word processor (*have* and *because*, in my case!), go to *Tools*, *Autocorrect* and type in both the way you regularly type them (wrongly) and also the correct way. The processor will then automatically correct your spelling. But remember that this does nothing for your own ability to spell!

Questions

In the sentences below, some words appear in four different spellings. One is correct. Identify the correct one in each case.

1. One of my aims is to help the children to become more (**independant, indeppendant, independent, independint**) of me, especially at break-times.

2. The problem with my aims is that they must be (**demonstratable, demonstrateable, demonstrabel, demonstrable**) as well as written down.

3. One of the fundamentals for me is careful and regular (**assesment, ascessment, assessment, asessment**) of the children, of their work as well as their interest in each other's trainers.

4. Some Y6 children had the demeanour of streetwise (**adolecents, adolesents, adolescents, adolessents**) but the social skills of the latest arrivals in the nursery.

5. Although some of my friends already want to (**persue, pursuie, perssue, pursue**) a career into management levels, I have seen my Head with white hair at 30.

6. Luckily, my class this year responds very well to fairy (**storys, storis, stories, storyes**), some based on their reasons for arriving late for school.

7. Another activity that they enjoyed was simply (**weighing, wieghing, weighting, wheighing**) ingredients for the recipe that led to that year's longest and largest absentee rate.

8 The class's enthusiasm for finding excuses to climb on the nursery roof (**fuelled, fueled, fuled, feulled**) my own for outdoor sports.

9. Nothing, not even the day that they upset a pot of glue on the gerbil, could (**effect, afect, efect, affect**) my liking for the class.

10. I became consumed with a sense of (**responsibility, ressponability, ressponibilty, responsibility**) for the class, despite their ignoring my safety instructions on our visit to the canal lock.

11. On my last teaching (**practisce, practise, practice, practiss**), I planned for everything except what actually happened.

12. With experience, I find that my anxieties (**dissappear, disappear, disapear, dissapear**) as easily as my memory of college.

13. Nobody who (**posesses, posseses, possesses, poseses**) the least sense could ignore the coincidence of parents' evening, an Ofsted visit and arson.

14. Though somewhat daunted by the apparent (**unpracticability, unpracticibility, unpractacability, impracticability, unpracticabality**) of my proposed Y3 overnight trek across the Brecon Beacons, I nevertheless put my case to the Head.

15. In preparation for the trek, the class underwent (**rigourous, rigerous, rigouros, rigorous**) training in falling down and not getting up.

16. Regrettably, there were some children who chose to (**exxagerate, exagerate, exagerrate, exaggerate**) the problems of night-time ridge-walking in the snow.

17. (**Regretably, regreatably, regrettably, reggrettably**), some parents chose to take the side of the children.

18. My (**automattic, automatick, automatic, automattick**), if guilty, response was to offer to produce the Christmas play for the school.

19. That not only pleased the parents but also caused them to tear up their (**pettition, petision, petiscion, petition**) to the governors.

20. Fortunately, that (**gaffe, gafe, gaff, gaph**) has taught me that teaching requires a rather greater maturity than those I teach.

21. A colleague in her (**fifth, fith, fitfth, figth**) year of teaching tried to console me by confessing that, in her first year, she was once late in submitting the register.

22. At least, that (**a loud, aloud, allowed, alowed**) me to throw sense as well as enthusiasm into the job.

23. There was no more talk of who would (**supercede, superseed, superscede, supersede**) me in the coveted role of Christmas play producer.

24. All in all, I approach the end of my first year in teaching with the (**maturity, matturity, maturaty, maturety**) that nobody at home ever expected of me.

25. After that first year, my father introduced me to the (**meadicinal, medisinal, medicinal, meddicinal**) benefits of sobriety and early nights.

2 | Punctuation

Introduction

15 marks are available for punctuation. That is half way to the pass mark.

Punctuation has often been undervalued yet its importance in conveying your meaning to a reader clearly and unambiguously is great. Poor punctuation can lead to the reader getting a quite false impression, as in:

The worst teachers spend their time doing nothing; the best sport.

if what you meant was:

The worst teachers spend their time doing nothing; the best, sport.

In this second example, the comma represents the 'missing' (or elliptical) phrase *spend their time doing* because a comma can be used to avoid repeating a stretch of language.

A literate teacher may need to check his or her spelling often but is, by definition, able to use punctuation well.

The aspects of punctuation in the test are concerned with ways in which writers mark off *units of meaning* (such as a sentence), ways in which the actual status of the language being used is clarified and ways in which words themselves are punctuated.

Punctuation to mark units of meaning

Any text is made up of parts: the whole text, the paragraphs, the sentences, the clauses and the phrases. These are the units of meaning greater than the individual word. The main ways in which we mark off where one unit ends and another begins are:

- **paragraph;**
- **full stop;**
- **comma.**

None of these is straightforward; all are partly a matter of personal style. Consequently, the key is to be consistent with punctuation within any one text.

Paragraph

A paragraph is a group of one or more sentences that have enough related meaning, enough similarity in content or topic, to form a group. The writer decides where to begin and end each paragraph, depending on how he or she regards the main groups of meaning. A good text is divided along consistent lines, following the same idea about what makes a chunk of meaning, and one sentence within the paragraph states the main idea. This is the topic sentence; it often comes first.

Good paragraphing also makes considered use of sentence adverbs, those connectives, such as *However, Furthermore, On the other hand, Fortunately,* etc., that link the meaning of the new paragraph to the previous one.

The test might show you a text that could have paragraphs but that is printed without any and might ask you to identify where paragraph boundaries could come.

Full stop

Full stops define a sentence, literally, by showing its limit. You need to develop a sense of what a sentence is to use full stops properly. If the largest unit of meaning is the unbroken, complete text and the next largest is the paragraph, the largest below that is the sentence. As a rule, it is one or more clauses long, has a sense of relative completeness about it and usually has a verb and its subject.

Over 80 per cent of all the punctuation marks used in British English are full stops and commas.

> **HINT** To help you to get a better grip of sentences and their need for a final full stop, look at *Clause, Sentence* and *Verb* in the Glossary. Keep that in mind as you read about commas.

Comma

It is not a simple task to use commas well. The first and simplest guidance is:

if you are not sure whether to use a comma or a full stop, use a full stop and begin a new sentence.

> *It was just what I had been looking for, from my experience with the previous class I felt a need for children who wanted to learn.*

should be:

> *It was just what I had been looking for. From my experience with the previous class, I felt a need for children who wanted to learn.*

Commas help us to separate items in a list. They can, therefore, be used as an alternative to the word *and* but not as well as *and*:

> *Above all, I like to teach music, dance, art and history.*

You do not need a comma after *art* because *and* here does the job of a comma. This could be written using *and* instead of a comma:

> *Above all, I like to teach music and dance and art and history.*

Sometimes, we use a phrase or word at the beginning of a sentence and then start to write what we mean.

The sentence at the bottom of page 17 is an example: it begins with *sometimes* and then continues with the subject of the sentence, *we*. Put a comma after that word or phrase before continuing with what you want to say. Apart from that *sometimes*, other common **sentence-openers,** or sentence adverbs, are:

On the other hand,
However,
Suddenly,
Next,
Instead,
Unfortunately,

Sometimes, we want to vary what we say by changing the order in which we say things. This might be because we want to *emphasise* something or other:

My last tutor asked if he could copy my maths plans because he felt that they were a good model.

This could be turned round without changing, adding or omitting any words but by adding a comma at the break:

Because he felt that they were a good model, my last tutor asked if he could copy my maths plans.

This is a rather tricky use of the comma. It can be important because it tells the reader precisely what the meaning is. The use of commas can put an end to *ambiguity*. This comma-free sentence is ambiguous:

The teachers who live in Gotham are all over six feet tall.

As it stands, this seems very improbable. But suppose the sentence is just about a group of people over six feet who simply happen to live in Gotham. That is more than probable. The fact that they live in Gotham is almost an afterthought. The essence of the sentence, the main clause, is:

The teachers are all over six feet tall.

Now, an extra, incidental bit of information is given. It is a relative clause:

who live in Gotham

This extra clause can be **embedded** (set inside) in the main clause. To show that it is extra, it is separated from the rest by commas:

The teachers, who live in Gotham, are all over six feet tall.

(This use of the embedded clause is a sophistication that the devisers of the Primary National Strategy would like to see promoted in schools.)

Not only clauses are embedded. We embed phrases and single words. They may appear at the beginning of a sentence (see the opening sentence adverbs above), in the middle

or at the end. Children can be helped by having a discussion about what to embed in a sentence (if anything) and where in the sentence the embedded item might go:

Naturally, the choice of where to apply was rather limited.

or:

The choice of where to apply was rather limited, naturally.

or:

The choice of where to apply was, naturally, rather limited.

The embedded item is bounded by a capital letter and a comma at the beginning of the sentence, by a comma and a full stop at the end and by two, paired commas in the middle.

When we write *dialogue*, a comma ends the text before the quotation marks and the spoken words begin:

She said, 'Come along with me, children.'

What commas cannot do is end a sentence.

Here are some other ways to mark units of meaning in a text: the **colon**, **semicolon**, **question mark** and **brackets**.

Colon

The commonest use of the colon is to introduce a list:

The children brought a wealth of evidence from the playground: sweet wrappers, milk straws, cards to swap, crisp packets and some cigarette packets.

Another use is to introduce some reasoning or evidence to support the part of the sentence that comes before the colon:

Some of them blamed the secondary school children: they reminded the class that several teenagers regularly took a short cut across their playground.

Semicolon

The semicolon is rarely used in the writing of many people; not only students and teachers but some of our greatest writers ignore this mark. It is possible to write without using it but it can allow a writer to put two independent clauses together that could stand as individual sentences but that the writer feels are unusually closely related. This book contains examples in its text.

Another use of the semicolon is to mark off items in a list following a colon, especially if the items in the list are each several words long:

The school still had some problems: a falling roll; two teachers due to retire within the year; an imminent Ofsted inspection.

However, commas can also do that job. Be careful: if one of those items has so many words that the phrase itself needs a comma, all the items must be separated by a semicolon.

Question mark

This mark ends a sentence that asks a question:

Are your reports nearly ready?

Will we need supply cover for next Tuesday?

It is not necessary at the end of a sentence that implies a question but that has the structure of a statement (that is, the subject comes before the verb):

I wonder if there will be any supply teachers available.
I asked him when he would be ready for swimming.

If the sentence is within quotation marks, the question mark comes before the final quotation mark:

'Can we get together about this Performance Management meeting?'
'Could you tell me why your assignment is 3,000 words over the limit?'

Brackets or parentheses

These marks (the two words really mean the same) begin and end an aside in a sentence. Often, a writer composes a sentence but wants to add something to it that is not strictly part of the sentence; rather, it is almost an afterthought or something that he or she would like to say as well as the sentence:

Not many of us (at least, not those under 60) can remember what it was like to teach in those controversial sixties.

We have had no child statemented (none that we were successful in having statemented, anyway!) for over five years now.

HINT   Look at *Parenthesis* in the Glossary.

Punctuation which indicates the status of the language being used

Speech marks (double quotes) and quotation marks (single quotes) can help you to make it clear to the reader that this or that piece of your writing is to be read in a particular way. Both can be, and are, in some published texts, used to mark **direct speech**, such as the dialogue in a story.

You might scribe a story for the class. Any dialogue, words actually spoken by a character, will need to be put inside **speech marks**:

When Fergus the king asked Nes to be his wife, she replied, "Only if I get something in return."

"What is that?" he asked.

Quotation marks can be used for the same purpose but they are valuable in their own right. They can draw the reader's attention to the way that some word or phrase sits oddly in the text as a whole:

The Director of Education said that anyone who rejected the proposal for closing two undersubscribed schools had to be 'doolally'.

They help the reader to see that a part of the text actually comes from some source other than the writer:

I have high hopes of getting a good job because my last Head said that I was 'as competent as most teachers are after a year or two of experience'.

They tell the reader that some of the text is the name of a film or the title of a book:

My friend started to read 'Harry Potter and the Goblet of Fire' but the spiders scared her so she stopped.

> **HINT**   Parentheses, speech marks and quotation marks all work in pairs. If the test shows just one parenthesis or speech/quotation mark, you know that there has to be another. Look for where it might be.

Punctuation within words

Hyphens, **apostrophes** and **capital letters** occur within single words; their job is to give the reader information about that word, not to show how larger units of meaning are organised or bounded.

Hyphens

Hyphens link two words that have another meaning when they occur together. Some of the first elements are words in themselves, others are abbreviations or suffixes:

well-stocked, ex-Head, post-Ofsted, pro-uniform, U-turn, T-shirt

This sort of hypenated word is a kind of half-way point between two words and one.

Apostrophe

The apostrophe, a minefield for some writers, has two main uses but is sometimes wrongly used for a third purpose.

First, **abbreviation.** When we write, we sometimes choose to leave letters out of words to get closer to the way we speak English. Because we rarely sound the full value of *we will, we do not, we shall not, we cannot*, we may abbreviate them:

we'll, don't, shan't, can't

One of the trickiest of these abbreviations is the use of *it's,* easily confused with *its*. The solution is simply never to write *it's*. *It's* is always an abbreviation, usually of *it is* but sometimes of *it has*. Abbreviations are normal in informal writing but unknown in formal texts. Only use *it's* when you mean to write an informal text and when you mean either *it is* or *it has*:

It's appropriate to write formally.

means the same as:

It is appropriate to write formally.

It's become obvious that clear writing matters.

means the same as:

It has become obvious that clear writing matters.

You will then write *its* only without an apostrophe and only when it is appropriate: as the direct equivalent of *her* or *his* before a noun:

The new Teaching Assistant put down her bag, helped Nathan out of his wheelchair and covered its seat with a cushion.

Only use the apostrophe as abbreviation when you feel quite confident and in control as a writer.

> **HINT** Never write *it's*. Write *it is* or *it has* instead and you can forget that apostrophe problem.

Second, **possession**. Books have titles. Write down who or what *possesses* the titles:

the book

then put an apostrophe:

the book'

and ask: does this word end with the letter *s*? If not, add one:

the book's

and continue:

the book's title.

If there are several books, you would have the sequence:

the books

then put an apostrophe

the books'

and ask: does this word end with the letter *s*? If it does, leave it alone:

the books'

and continue:

the books' titles.

There is no need to think about singular or plural provided you place the apostrophe before you check if the word ends in *s* or not. Of course, the way this works means that, in most cases, the placing of the apostrophe does say whether the word before is singular or plural but that does not always help. If men have ambitions and you want to write about that affliction, the singular and plural – *man* and *men* – would look like this:

the man	*the men*
the man'	*the men'*
the man's	*the men's*
the man's ambitions	*the men's ambitions*

Third, **the wrong use of the apostrophe plus s as a plural form**. The sight of cards on market stalls saying *Cabbage's* and *Cauli's* (and *Ca'fe* in one town) has led to the rather unfair name of *Greengrocers' Apostrophe* for this wrong use of *'s* instead of the simple plural **s**.

There is a special, and wrong, case of the apostrophe-as-plural that goes far beyond the efforts of any greengrocer. We now have quite a few words in English that end with a vowel, especially o. *Video, studio, radio, data, scampi, criteria*, etc. Some people add *'s* to these words to indicate a plural: *video's*, etc. There is no need. Most simply add an *es*: *radioes*; but so many people make them plural by simply adding *s* (the commonest way of making plurals in English) that either is acceptable and you might choose to use the easier *s*.

Capital letters

A capital letter is always needed at the beginning of a new sentence:

Only in my wildest dreams could I have succeeded in obtaining a post in such a school.

It is needed for titles and proper nouns: the names of people and places:

The letter from the Headteacher, Mrs Pendlebury, welcomed me to Ordsall.

There is no need to use a capital for *headteacher* if there is no name to follow.

Questions

Like all the tests, this one is computerised. Details of what you do in the test and how you do it are on pages 1–5, but it will also help you a lot to look at the TDA website www.tda.gov.uk/skillstests/literacy.aspx. If you want to change anything, that can be done.

The test will present you with a text from which much of the punctuation has been deleted. Your task is to create a properly punctuated complete text from this incomplete one. The key thing, again, is consistency: read the text and its existing punctuation as information about how to complete it.

The passages below are examples of the kind of test you will have.

Since you are doing this test in a book and not on a computer, read the whole passage and add any punctuation you feel is necessary in pencil or by making a note. Where you want to change a lower case to a capital letter, put a circle round the letter and write *cap* in the margin; where you want a new paragraph, put a forward slash (/) immediately before the first word of the new paragraph and write *np* in the margin.

1. As soon as we speak we reveal a great deal of ourselves to our audience. Suppose you ask someone,

   "shall we have a drink

   Suppose the other person replies

   "Yes, I'd like a whiskey me."

   That tag, *me*, tells you that the speaker probably comes from manchester.

   Sometimes, what people say does tell you something about their origin but it is less definite. A friend asks you and another friend,

   "Now, what would youse two like to drink?"

   The questioner may or may not come from Ireland but will certainly have a background there because that use of 'youse', unknown in standard English, has its roots in the Irish having one form of 'you' for one person tú and another form of 'you' for two people sibh. Of course, none of this means that any of these speakers could actually speak any Irish.

2. If we look at boys performance in English, we have to agree that there is, generally some cause for concern. Is there anything that can be done to help them to improve?

   Among the approaches that seemed to help boys in their reading are

   enthusiastically encouraged private reading;

   clearly-set tasks

   explicit teaching of reading strategies;

   a wide range of outcomes from reading;

   reading preferences that are discussed.

   The dfee's anxiety was evident in the QCA report Can Do Better.' However its analysis of the situation was coupled with extremely supportive case studies that suggest helpful shortterm plans and long-term strategies.

3. What is it about standard English that makes it standard Like every language, English has gone through many changes. The Saxons and Angles who settled here

brought their own languages with them predominantly Saxon, and after a while the dialects of Anglo-Saxon overcame the Celtic languages that had flourished along with Latin until soon after the Romans left in 410 AD. The languages spoken by the later Scandinavian invaders were probably just about intelligible to some of the Anglo Saxons but changes and borrowings continued: the new invaders legacy to us includes **they, them, their**. Anglo-Saxon, modified by Scandinavian, with dialects that were barely intelligible to other Anglo-Saxon speakers, continued for hundreds of years but, thankfully it became simpler The German word for **big** is **gross** but it has six versions. Our Anglo-Saxon ancestors had eleven versions of adjectives we have just three: **big, bigger, biggest**. Even when we complicate matters by having **good, better best,** that is still easier than Anglo-Saxon.

3 | Grammar

Introduction

10 marks are available for grammar.

One of the main jobs of a teacher is to work with colleagues in producing documents for a variety of audiences, from known people within the school to outside bodies, and for a range of purposes, from planning teaching to explaining and presenting work that has been done. That collaboration involves drafting, redrafting and proof-reading. This test does not test your writing; rather, it will test:

- **your grasp of written standard English;**
- **your ability to identify and use it unambiguously;**
- **your understanding of which style is appropriate to the text in question.**

How will these three aspects of grammatical knowledge be tested? What, in detail, do those aspects mean you need to know?

The test presents you with a range of options and asks you to select the one that you think is most appropriate. In that way, it explores your ability to spot and change faults in written English and to identify the appropriate form. People who already use English competently and with confidence would not make such faults and would notice them in the writing of other people or, perhaps, in an early draft of their own work.

The items of grammatical knowledge that will be tested are set out and explained below.

Consistency with written standard English

Each test presents you with some examples of English; only one example is acceptable as standard English. You have to choose and identify that one. To be able to do that, you need to have an awareness of what kinds of error are possible, of the features of non-standard English, and of the appropriate, standard alternative.

This is the list of features of non-standard English that the test covers:

- **failure to observe sentence boundaries;**
- **abandoned or faulty constructions and sentence fragments;**
- **lack of cohesion;**
- **lack of agreement between subject and verb;**
- **should have/of, might have/of;**
- **inappropriate or incomplete verb forms;**
- **wrong or missing preposition, e.g. different from/than/to;**
- **noun/pronoun agreement error;**
- **determiner/noun agreement error;**
- **inappropriate or missing determiner;**
- **problems with comparatives and superlatives;**
- **problems with relative pronouns in subordinate clauses;**
- **inappropriate or missing adverbial forms.**

Failure to observe sentence boundaries

Perhaps the commonest failing in student-teachers' writing is this problem with deciding where a sentence ends and needs a full stop (see section on punctuation). Be very wary of sentences that go on and on. It is very easy to ignore that length and, worse still, the complexity that falls into the sentence as it develops. It is far better to write more sentences, varying in complexity, with some short, simple, one-clause sentences among them. For example:

It was my great opportunity, from my experience with the previous class I knew how to make the most of the first group's ideas.

Should be:

It was my great opportunity. From my experience with the previous class, I knew how to make the most of the first group's ideas.

Look at 'Commas' in the section on punctuation. Generally, unless you know you can write well, do not be too ambitious as a stylist. Your writing is more likely to be sound standard English if you follow the advice about short sentences. If you are not sure whether it should be a comma or a full stop, put a full stop. In most cases, you will be safe.

HINT   Use full stops more often.

Abandoned or faulty constructions and sentence fragments

A sentence should use consistent structures. It is very easy, especially if you write slowly, to lose track of the way you are writing, the structures you are using. The best way to avoid this problem is to reread what you write as you write and, particularly, to look out for any faults that you know you are prone to. Usually, the way that you begin the sentence is the way it should continue.

This is a **faulty construction**:

Concerned about the falling numbers in the city's schools so the Director of Education proposed that two primary schools should be closed and one re-opened as a junior school.

It should be either:

Concerned about the falling numbers in the city's schools, the Director of Education proposed that two primary schools should be closed and one re-opened as a junior school.

or:

The Director of Education proposed that two primary schools should be closed and one re-opened as a junior school because he was concerned about the falling numbers in the city's schools.

or:

> *Because he was concerned about the falling numbers in the city's schools, the Director of Education proposed that two primary schools should be closed and one re-opened as a junior school.*

This is a sentence fragment:

> *Although there was still uncertainty about the best choice of software.*

This has obviously become separated from the sentence of which it should be a part. In a sense, this is the other side of the previous problem with sentence boundaries: this time, the writer has probably put in an unnecessary full stop that cuts this fragment off from the rest. The whole sentence might have looked like this:

> *Although there was still uncertainty about the best choice of software, the Governors decided to go ahead with the purchase of new computers.*

Here, the full sentence is given and the whole is much easier to grasp. The word 'sentence' is notoriously difficult to define but those ideas of completeness and comprehensibility are central.

An alternative to that whole sentence would be:

> *The Governors decided to go ahead with the purchase of new computers although there was still uncertainty about the best choice of software.*

It is worth noting here, as in some other examples in this book, that there are often at least two ways to structure a sentence, often with little or no change to the words themselves. What has been altered here in the two acceptable alternatives is the sequence of the two clauses and the punctuation: if the minor (subordinate or dependent) clause comes first, separate it from the following main clause with a comma.

> **HINT** Get into the habit, when you read a text, of seeing if some of its sentences can be restructured.

Lack of cohesion

Most of us think of grammar as the way that words are combined to make phrases, clauses and sentences. In recent decades, a lot of attention has been paid to the way that sentences are also linked together so that we know that this series of sentences is one text, not a random collection from different texts. All of us automatically use a variety of ways to make our writing (and our speech) link together as a whole, to give it cohesion.

Lack of cohesion is what happens when the writer has not made the links between sentences – or within them – as clear as they would be if they were cohesive. Cohesion deals with the various ways in which writers create these clear links. The test focuses on one of these ways, the cohesive link that depends on the appropriate use of pronouns (see the section on punctuation, and *cohesion, connective* and *pronoun* in the glossary).

This short passage **lacks cohesion**:

> *A newly qualified **teacher** should receive good support from the school and from the LEA. **They** nevertheless have substantial responsibility.*

What is wrong here is that the noun *teacher* is singular but the pronoun that refers to it, *they,* is plural. This is a common error and can only be rectified by rereading as you write, checking each use of a pronoun and making sure that there is no ambiguity about which noun it refers to.

The two sentences above should read:

> *Newly qualified **teachers** should receive good support from the school and from the LEA. **They** nevertheless have substantial responsibility.*

Here, both the noun and its pronoun are plural. Sometimes the pronoun needs to be changed and sometimes, as here, it is easier to change the noun. It would be possible to revise the two problem sentences like this:

> *A newly-qualified **teacher** should receive good support from the school and from the LEA but would nevertheless have substantial responsibility.*

Here, there would be a problem in choosing a pronoun because English has only *he* or *she*, neither of which is acceptable here. One way to get round this little problem is to leave out the pronoun altogether, as the sentence above shows. That omission of a word that would normally be present is another kind of **cohesive device**: ellipsis.

Lack of agreement between subject and verb

This is another very common error. It can show itself in many ways:

- **two nouns (e.g. *maths and English*) with a singular verb (e.g. *is*);**
- **plural determiner (e.g. *these*) with a singular verb (e.g. *was*);**
- **singular determiner (e.g. *this*) with a plural verb (e.g. *were*);**
- **singular verb (e.g. *is*) with some non-English plurals (e.g. *data*).**

Here are some examples of those four basic kinds of error.

Two nouns with a singular verb:

> *Underlying the good SAT results **was** the hard **work** of the pupils and a determined **staff**.*

This should be:

> *Underlying the good SAT results **were** the hard **work** of the pupils and a determined **staff**.*

The subject of the verb *was* is plural: *work* and *staff*; two nouns make a plural subject. If the subject is plural, the verb should be plural: *were*.

Plural determiner with a singular verb:

> *Some teachers who had been trained in ICT **has** made excellent use of word processing.*

Some is a plural determiner so it needs a plural verb: *have*, not *has*. That sentence should read:

> *Some teachers who had been trained in ICT **have** made best use of word processing.*

Singular determiner with a plural verb:

> *Many of us grew up with a very prescriptive view of language without realising that **that** view of grammar **were** inadequate.*

The second use of *that* is a singular determiner so it needs a singular verb: *was*, not *were*. That sentence should read:

> *Many of us grew up with a very prescriptive view of language without realising that **that** view of grammar **was** inadequate.*

As you probably noticed, most of these determiners can also function as pronouns.

Singular verb with some non-English plurals:

> *There was some argument about the findings because the research **criteria was** in dispute.*

The word *criteria* is a plural because it comes from Greek and follows a Greek way of forming plurals. The singular form is *criterion*. Since *criteria* is plural, the verb should be *were*:

> *There was some argument about the findings because the research **criteria were** in dispute.*

An equally safe version would be:

> *There was some argument about the findings because the research **criterion was** in dispute.*

Of course, the meanings of the two sentences would be different!

English uses many words that still have their original forms of singular and plural. Some people feel that, when they are used in English, those singular and plural forms should still be used. At the moment, for instance, it seems that there is still a useful distinction in English between *criterion* and *criteria* that is worth retaining. On the other hand, some foreign loan-words are known in English in either, predominantly, a plural form (for example, *graffiti, agenda, data*) or a singular form (for example, *rhododendron*). Few of us talk of *graffito* or *rhododendra* for the simple reason that we do not know the Italian or Greek plurals (and, if we did, who – or whom – would we talk to?).

All language changes and that applies to standard English as well as to other varieties. It is likely that words like *data* will settle down as singular forms because nobody else uses them as plural. Perhaps *data* itself will become both singular and plural, rather like *sheep*. *Criterion* and *criteria* are easier words to use confidently because both are used quite widely in British English. The point about using standard English is to use the variety of it that is being used and understood currently.

This degree of uncertainty also applies to some other parts of this book. You will find at least as much uncertainty about these and other matters in Bill Bryson's helpful book, *Troublesome Words*.

Of all the words that still use their original, foreign plural forms, *data* and *criteria* are probably the ones most likely to be used by people in education.

Should have/of, might have/of

English makes a lot of use of modal verbs like *would, could, must, need not* and *ought to*, followed by the verb *have*. When we speak, we usually abbreviate *have* to a sound that we write as *'ve*. So we write *might have, should have*, etc. It is always wrong to write *of* in these constructions. It is always right to write *have*.

> In the headteacher's view, the school might not **of** been put under Special Measures if the stable staffing the school had benefited from earlier had been maintained.

This should read:

> In the headteacher's view, the school might not **have** been put under Special Measures if the stable staffing the school had benefited from earlier had been maintained.

It is always worth bearing in mind that written standard English is different from any spoken English in many ways and that it is not safe to rely too much on the sounds that are spoken as a guide to the way that the words are written. Nobody pronounces the last letter in *comb* but most of us put it in when we write the word.

Inappropriate or incomplete verb forms

One recommendation that is made repeatedly in this book is to reread what you write as you write. Even good writers can make embarrassing mistakes if they do not check what they write (this is being written by someone who consistently typed *the* as *teh* until he persuaded the Tools/Autocorrect facility to sort it out automatically). Whole words can be missed out, especially if the writer's attention is focused on another bit of the content. You need to be aware of this tendency that we all have and to pay particular attention to a fairly common error: the verb form that is either not appropriate or that is missing altogether.

> Most of the class had learned use the spell check by half-term.

This should read:

> Most of the class had learned **to** use the spell check by half-term.

One possible factor affecting this problem is that there are constructions in American English that do omit the word *to*: for example, *That afternoon, the class decided to **go explore** the neighbouring building site.* In British English, the word *to* would be used: *That afternoon, the class decided to **go to explore** the neighbouring building site.* The test is based on British English.

Sometimes, the verb itself gets left out:

Later, most of the children to show their findings to the head.

This should read:

*Later, most of the children **wanted** to show their findings to the head.*

It should be obvious that *wanted* is not the only verb that could fit this space but some verb, in an appropriate tense, is certainly needed.

> **HINT**   This is one area where, as a writer, you can rely on the way you use language when speaking.

Wrong or missing preposition, e.g. different from/than/to

Words like *with, near, to, towards, through, in, by,* etc. are prepositions. They are usually found between two nouns (*a cat **on** a mat*) a verb and a noun (*a cat sat **on** a mat*) or some other part of speech and a noun or pronoun (*older **than***.) Despite what was said above, there are some bits of language that change very slowly, if at all, and prepositions are among them. We still use the same prepositions that our ancestors used centuries ago. Prepositions are a *closed* word class.

The problem with them – and it is a problem; adult users of English probably have more trouble with prepositions than with any other part of speech – is that it is very easy to use an inappropriate one. This can alter what we are trying to say and cause misunderstanding.

There are some prepositions that use more than one word: complex prepositions, such as *different from*. An alternative to this is *different to*. At the moment, the complex preposition *different than* is considered to be non-standard English. In that case, do not use it in formal writing; that is, in most writing.

The performance of this year's Y2 class was quite different than last year's.

should be either:

The performance of this year's Y2 class was quite different from last year's.

or:

The performance of this year's Y2 class was quite different to last year's.

Noun/pronoun agreement error

If you substitute pronouns for nouns in these sentences, you will notice a change in the pronouns but not in the nouns:

The man liked the woman.

becomes:

He liked her.

The woman liked the man.

becomes:

She liked him.

Two nouns have become four pronouns.

Aloysius assaulted the entire staff of the school.

becomes:

He assaulted them.

The entire staff of the school wanted to exclude Aloysius.

becomes:

They wanted to exclude him.

Man, woman, Aloysius, entire staff of the school all remained the same wherever they were in the sentences and whatever job they were doing. Nouns do not change according to position and job (although they can take a plural *s/es* and a possessive *'s* or *s'*.) On the other hand, pronouns change a lot:

I	*me*	*my*	*mine*	*myself*
you	*you*	*your*	*yours*	*yourself*
she	*her*	*her*	*hers*	*herself*
he	*him*	*his*	*his*	*himself*
It	*it*	*its*	*its*	*itself*
we	*us*	*our*	*ours*	*ourselves*
they	*them*	*their*	*theirs*	*themselves*

Some years ago, the Prime Minister of the day rejected criticisms 'about Mr Lamont and I'. That is a very common error that is easy to avoid if you ask yourself what you would put if Mr Lamont were not involved. Would you write or say:

about I

or would you say:

about me

The basic rule is to ignore the *he and/him and* bits and to ask yourself: 'Would I use *I* here or would I use *me*'? So, just as you would almost certainly write:

I have an interview in Wythenshawe next week.

You should also write:

My friend and I have interviews in Wythenshawe next week.

As you would almost certainly write:

The head showed me round the school.

You should also write:

The head showed my friend and me round the school.

To write:

The head showed my friend and I round the school.

is an unusual example of non-standard English, unusual because it is not the English of working-class users but that spoken by middle- or aspiring middle-class users of English who believe that the *he and I* form seems more acceptable. It isn't.

Try to remember a simple sentence, such as:

I love my mother.

The word *I* comes before the verb *love* and, because it comes before the verb in this very simple sentence, it is the subject of the verb and of the sentence. If you write:

My mother loves me.

the subject is *My mother*. You do not do the loving, you *are* the loved. You are the object of the verb and of the sentence. *I* is different from *me* because it has a different meaning and does a different job.

Determiner/noun agreement error

In a radio broadcast some years ago, the then Secretary of State for Education referred to:

Those sort of programmes.

This is the error that happens when you get confused about how to link a determiner – words like *all, some, three, many, that, those, my, the, a/an* – to its noun. Such errors happen most often in brief phrases followed by a verb. This sentence-opening is acceptable English:

determiner	noun phrase	verb ...
This	*type of error*	*is ...*

It is acceptable because the determiner and the verb are singular and so is the *headword* of the noun phrase, *type*. You need to know which word in the phrase is the headword, the real centre of the phrase. If the headword is singular, the verb and the determiner should also be singular. If the headword is plural, the verb and the determiner should also be plural. It is common to find sentences like this:

> *Although drafting and redrafting have been requirements since the 1989 National Curriculum in English, these kinds of activity is stumbling blocks for many children.*

This should be:

> *Although drafting and redrafting have been requirements since the 1989 National Curriculum in English, these kinds of activity are stumbling blocks for many children.*

This error, which is far more widespread in speech, is easy to understand but it is still not acceptable as standard English. The writer has been trapped into using the singular verb *is* because the nearest word that *looks* like a subject – but is not – is the singular noun *activity*. In noun-phrases like:

> *sorts of book*
> *kinds of poetry*
> *types of text*

the headword in every case is a plural: *sorts, kinds, types*. That plural headword is followed by a preposition and a singular noun. The next word is likely to be a verb and, in standard English, the verb has to agree with the headword of the noun phrase; that is, if the headword is plural, the verb should be plural, too.

So should the determiner.

Inappropriate or missing determiner

The singular determiners *this, that* and the plural determiners *these, those* are also called demonstrative pronouns. We said earlier that many determiners also act as pronouns.

If you were writing about your plans for the next half-term, you might begin:

> *Next term, I need to make sure that **the** key points of our work in **the** Literacy Strategy have been taken on board.*

You would not – and should not – begin:

> *Next term, I need to make sure that **those** key points of our work in **that** Literacy Strategy have been taken on board.*

What is wrong about the second usage is that the determiners *those* and *that* refer back to something that has already been said and this is the opening so nothing has been said. *The* is wholly appropriate in this case because it introduces and establishes what you are going to write about.

Problems with comparatives and superlatives

The computer that this is being written on is new but it is not as new as the one my friend recently bought. His computer is *newer*. He says that his son, being something of an expert in these matters, has just bought a computer that is so new that nothing newer exists! That computer is – for the moment – the newest.

We are all used to making comparisons between things and people. In standard English, this is done by using one of the two comparative forms: add *-er* to an adjective, as happened with *new/newer,* or precede it with *more,* as with *more recent.* If we want to state the ultimate in such a series, it is superlative: superlatives are expressed by adding *-est,* as with *newest,* or by preceding the adjective with *most,* as in *most recent.*

In most cases, it makes sense to write sentences that contain comparatives or superlatives but not both.

> *If children are put into groups according to whatever seating arrangements suit the activity best, the result seems to be a class that is **calmest** and **more attentive**.*

This should be:

> *If children are put into groups according to whatever seating arrangements suit the activity best, the result seems to be a class that is **calmer** and **more attentive**.*

It is hard to imagine a situation where it would be appropriate to write *calmer and most attentive.* To avoid this, simply reread it yourself and ask if it feels as though it makes good sense.

Since the comparison between the computers mentioned earlier obviously depended on there being another computer to compare with the first, it was necessary to bring in a third computer to see which was the newest. Superlatives are used when three or more things are being compared and comparatives when two only are being compared. Yet it is common to write or say sentences like:

> *Timothy is the **tallest** twin.*

This should be:

> *Timothy is the **taller** twin.*

There are only two twins so a comparative form of *tall* is all that is needed.

> **HINT** Alice is tall; Lucy is the taller of the *two*; Annie and Joe are the smallest of the four cousins. Compare two, it's *taller*; three or more, one will be *tallest*.

Problems with relative pronouns in subordinate clauses

First, we will go over **subordinate clauses**.

Suppose you write a simple sentence, with one clause, a main clause; something like this:

I still need some information about my new class.

You can say something more, perhaps about why you need that information; something like this:

I still need some information about my new class so that I can plan to help them.

What you have added to that main clause is another one, subordinate to it, that is called, reasonably enough, a subordinate clause. It needs the main clause to make full sense. It is a clause because it has a verb – *can plan* – and a subject – *I*.

Next, look at **relative pronouns**. These are pronouns that can introduce a subordinate clause. Most subordinate clauses are introduced by connectives such as **and, so that, because, if, unless, although**. Some, however, are introduced by a pronoun. These relative pronouns refer back to a noun in the main clause. The relative pronouns are:

who, whom, which, that

They appear in sentences like these:

*The head believed that the school needed a teacher **who** could develop ICT work.*

*After a lot of discussion, the interviewing panel agreed to appoint the candidate **whom** the head preferred.*

*The Chair of the interviewing panel restated the criteria **which** they had drawn up.*

*The result of the interviews was one **that** the whole panel was happy with.*

It is also possible to leave out the relative pronoun in many cases. This sentence:

*She was the one **whom** they wanted.*

could also be written as:

*She was the one **that** they wanted.*

but also as:

She was the one they wanted.

The likely error that some fall into is to use a relative pronoun that is not appropriate. **Which** is the pronoun we use when we are dealing with inanimate things. It is appropriate in this sentence:

*Over the term, the class had read texts **which** really extended their range of interests and abilities.*

It is not appropriate in this sentence because teachers are not inanimate:

*They had chosen the teacher **which** the head wanted.*

That should be either:

>   *They had chosen the teacher **whom** the head wanted.*

or:

>   *They had chosen the teacher the head wanted.*

When do you use **who** and when do you use **whom**? It is the same question as whether to use **he** or **him, she** or **her, I** or **me, we** or **us**. Suppose you are writing a very formal piece and you try the two options in this sentence:

>   *The panel chose the candidate **who/whom** was best.*

Ask yourself whether you would be more likely to write:

>   *She was best*

or:

>   *Her was best.*

Unless you have a very unusual and inadequate grasp of English, you would say *She was best*. That means you would choose *who*. On the other hand, if you wanted to write this sentence:

>   *The head asked the rest of the panel **who/whom** they liked.*

You could ask yourself whether it would make more sense to write:

>   *They liked she.*

or:

>   *They liked her.*

You would choose *her* and so you would also choose *whom*.

Although many of us hardly ever use *whom,* the test is based on formal writing and does expect it to be used.

Inappropriate or missing adverbial forms

Sometimes, we can confuse the use of an adjective and an adverb. We know that we can write:

>   *She was a fast runner.*

where *fast* is an adjective, rather like *quick*. However, we can also write:

>   *She ran fast.*

where *fast* is an adverb, just like *quickly*. We know that many adverbs do not end in *-ly*. This very reliable bit of knowledge might tempt some of us to write sentences like this, where an adjective is used instead of an adverb:

On the whole, student options were intelligent chosen.

This should be:

On the whole, student options were intelligently chosen.

This is not the sort of error that native users of a language tend to make but it is the sort that can easily creep into a written text. That is why we repeatedly advise you to read and reread as you write. Get a feel for the sense and the flow of what you write and for the tone of voice you are using as a writer.

Sense, clarity and freedom from ambiguity

Some fiction and much poetry deliberately make very profitable use of the ambiguities and optional meanings that can be made from language. Most writing, however, has to make clarity a priority. Make your writing as easy to read as possible; change anything that is ambiguous; check it all the time to make sure that it makes sense.

You will be tested on your ability to spot when a piece of writing is clear and when it is not. This means that you need to have a good idea of the place that grammar can play in helping a text to be clear. The test will show you examples of writing and ask you to identify which of several options would make the piece clear.

These are some of the factors that make writing unclear:

Lack of coherence

Some texts are easier to read than others. If it is easy to understand, it must be coherent: it has *coherence*; the bits hold together to make a whole. Writers use a variety of ways to make this happen; for example, that pronoun *this* refers back to the idea of coherence in the previous sentence. Pronouns are crucial in making links *between* sentences in a continuous text.

Writers use other devices to make clauses hold together *within* a sentence. For example, they use *connectives* so that one clause can be linked in meaning to another; in this sentence, *so that* is a connective, linking *they use connectives* to its subordinate clause. That use of grammatical devices to create that coherence is called *cohesion*.

In the test, you will be asked to identify when a text lacks coherence because there are problems with:

- **tense;**
- **unrelated participles; or**
- **an ambiguous use of pronouns.**

These are all explained below.

Wrong tense or tense inconsistency

Tense is the aspect of a verb that deals with time. It is possible to use more than one tense in one sentence, as in this:

*My father **was** a sheet-metal worker, I **am** a teacher and my daughter **is going to be** a teacher.*

The first verb, *was,* is a form of the past tense; the second, *am,* is a form of the present; the third, *is going to be,* is a form of the future tense.

Other forms of the past include *has been, used to be.* Other forms of the present include *am being* (with verbs other than **be,** the present can also use *do,* as in *do like, do care,* etc.). Other forms of the future include *will be.*

There is no problem with the use of different tenses in that simple sentence. That is because the meaning of the sentence really is about different times so it is right to use different tenses. The key to all this is to keep a close eye on what you mean to write, what tense fits what you are trying to say. Keep rereading and checking! If you do, you are less likely to use tenses inconsistently, the commonest failing with this aspect of written grammar.

> **HINT** Over time, you will strengthen your grasp of tense if you read fairly quickly. Slow readers – and writers – easily lose track of what happens when.

*Liam began his book at half-term and **finishes** it last week.*

should be:

*Liam began his book at half-term and **finished** it last week.*

Began and *finished* are both verbs in the past tense. That fits the meaning of the sentence and is therefore consistent. It would also be consistent if the truth was this:

Liam began his book at half-term and will finish it next week.

There, *began* is in the past tense and *will finish* is in the future tense but the sentence is grammatically consistent because it fits the meaning.

A sentence such as:

*The staff will have written their reports by Friday and so **met** the deadline.*

should be:

*The staff will have written their reports by Friday and so **will meet** the deadline.*

In the first sentence, the staff have not yet completed the reports so it is not true to say they have already met a deadline. That does not make sense and so is inconsistent.

Unrelated participles

What are participles and in what ways might they be unrelated? In a sentence such as:

The school had closed for Easter.

the word *closed* follows a subject, the noun *school,* and immediately follows a form of the verb *to have.* A word that could do that is a **participle**, a part of the verb which expresses tense (in this case, a form of the past tense). Past participles often end in *-ed* but may end in *-en* (*written*) *-n* (*shown*) *-d* (*read*) or *-t* (*thought*).

In a sentence such as:

The school is closing for Easter.

the word *closing* follows a subject, the noun *school,* and immediately follows a form of the verb *to be.* Therefore, *closing* is also a participle and it expresses a form of the present tense.

A participle never has a subject, such as the pronouns *I, you, she, he, it, we, they,* immediately before it; the verb *to be* or *to have* has to come between them, as in the examples above.

Participles can be found in some clauses of this type:

Collaborating with someone who has more competence, a learner can be helped to construct new meanings.

In that sentence, the question of who does the *collaborating* is answered by the subject of the next clause: *the learner.* That is an example of a *related participle*; the participle is unambiguously related to a subject. However, the participle is not related to the subject in a sentence like this:

Collaborating with someone who has more competence, the teacher can help the learner to construct new meanings.

Here, the subject of that second clause is the teacher but the person who collaborates with someone who has more competence is the learner. The participle, *collaborating*, is *unrelated* to the subject, *the teacher.*

Unrelated participles are unacceptable because they are confusing and may be ambiguous. They should be avoided.

The sentence:

Being well-managed, the head of Armitage School could afford to employ a 0.5 teaching assistant after Christmas.

is unacceptable because it is the school that is well-managed, not the head.

The sentence:

> *Providing far more than the national average of free dinners, Seddon Junior School might be expected to have considerable problems.*

is acceptable because there is no doubt that it is the school that provides many free dinners.

Attachment ambiguities

Always keep an eye on the meaning of what you write or read. This book stresses that again and again but it is clear from what many people write that this advice is easily overlooked.

For example, if you wrote:

> *The headteacher told me about the exclusion appeal.*

you could add to that sentence a phrase about when the appeal was to be held. Where would that phrase appear? If you wrote:

> ***On Monday,*** *the headteacher told me about the exclusion appeal.*

that states unambiguously that Monday was the day that you were told. If you wrote:

> *The headteacher told me about the exclusion appeal **on Monday**.*

the change of position now *implies* that the appeal will take place on Monday. The problem is that it still allows the reader to *infer* that Monday was when you heard about the appeal. Does the phrase **on Monday** refer to the verb *told* or to the noun *appeal*? One sentence has two possible meanings although one – the timing of the appeal – is the more likely because *appeal* and *on Monday* appear close to each other.

It is easy to avoid this ambiguity by turning that added two-word phrase into a clause, as in:

> *The headteacher told me about the exclusion appeal **that would take place on Monday**.*

Vague or ambiguous pronoun reference

This kind of ambiguity is very common. In children's writing, it is very common indeed. One of the best activities that teachers can demonstrate, model and encourage is how to redraft a piece of writing by checking that there is no ambiguity about which nouns the pronouns refer to. Unless children (and other writers!) write quickly enough to be able to keep in mind what they are writing as they write, and unless they check what they write, it is very likely that they will use pronouns such as *he, she, it, they* (and the other forms of the pronoun, such as *him, her, them,* etc.) in ways that do not refer clearly to their nouns.

*All the new computers and most of the stationery materials have been stored in the old stock cupboards. Nothing more can be done with **them** until the electrician arrives.*

should be:

All the new computers and most of the stationery materials have been stored in the old stock cupboards. Nothing more can be done with the computers until the electrician arrives.

Unless the computers are specified – and that means using the noun, not the pronoun – it seems as if the electrician has to do something with the stationery as well. This would be, at least, confusing.

Clarity matters and, therefore, so does explicitness: that means using nouns instead of pronouns if it would be confusing to do otherwise.

*Liam and Aloysius took Ryan and Nathan to see if **their** food was ready.*

should be:

Liam and Aloysius took Ryan and Nathan to see if all their food was ready.

or:

Liam and Aloysius took Ryan and Nathan to see if Liam's and Aloysius' food was ready.

or:

Liam and Aloysius took Ryan and Nathan to see if Ryan's and Nathan's food was ready.

Which you use depends on your meaning. Some of these seem clumsy but even clumsiness is better than confusion. This particular confusion is very common in children's writing.

Confusion of words, e.g. imply/infer

All varieties of all languages change all the time. That is the single most obvious fact about language. Using standard English does not mean using the language of a century or two ago if it is very different from usage today. On the other hand, many older usages are still widespread among literate users of English so you are advised still to follow that variety of standard English.

One usage that seems to be common can cause real problems with understanding. English has many words that look and sound rather alike and so are sometimes used interchangeably but their meanings are quite different. If you say to a fairly educated person that you are *disinterested* about the children you teach, you should get some approval because it means that you are impartial, not that you are uninterested. So:

*Just because I said I didn't mind teaching either Y3 or Y4, the head thinks I'm **disinterested**.*

should be:

> Just because I said I didn't mind teaching either Y3 or Y4, the head thinks I'm **uninterested**.

If you have no great preference, you really are *disinterested*!

> He **inferred** that I'm not bothered who I teach.

should be:

> He **implied** that I'm not bothered who [to be formal, whom] I teach.

The odd thing about this particular confusion is that the words are almost opposite. If you imply something to a friend, your friend should infer the same message from you. *Infer* means *conclude,* as in:

> From the way he was talking about falling roles, I **inferred** that there could be a redundancy soon.

Imply means *to suggest something without directly saying so,* as in:

> I know she didn't say definitely but she **implied** that she might have a job for me next term.

Here are some other words that are often confused:

Except in uncommon usages such as: *The staff room had been burgled when someone* **effected** *an entry from the playground side,* the word *effect* is used as a noun:

> Unexpectedly, the music had a calming **effect** on a usually unruly class.

Affect is almost always a verb, as in:

> Yes, the music definitely **affected** them strongly.

Rebut, refute and **deny** are sometimes used as though they were interchangeable. Their meanings are related but distinct:

> When I implied that the deputy had forgotten about the Theatre in Education visit, she **refuted** what I had said by showing me the letter she had written to book the visit.

Here, the deputy head proved that the implied accusation was wrong by providing evidence; she *refuted* it.

> She was angry and **rebutted** the accusation, calling me a nasty-minded trouble-maker who should think about a suitable job, such as pig-farming.

The deputy is more emotional and does not bother with the evidence.

> All she needed to do was to **deny** it.

The accuser now wishes that the deputy had restricted herself to a mere denial, without proving the point and without the anger. *Deny* can be an angry verb and it can involve proof but something else has to be added to make those points: *denied angrily, denied the accusation and showed the proof.*

Here are some other words that may get confused:

Discrete means not continuous; **discreet** means able to avoid embarrassing others – or yourself:

> *Some of his sentences were a list of **discrete** words, unconnected by any grammatical device.*

but:

> *There was so much rumour in the air that we all appreciated having such a **discreet** colleague.*

Accept means to receive something, particularly without fuss; **except** means that somebody or something is not part of a general situation:

> *The head **accepted** my apology and carried on conducting the assembly himself.*

but:

> *After the staff meeting, the head dismissed everybody **except** me.*

Contemptuous means that the subject feels contempt for somebody or something; **contemptible** is what that somebody or something is:

> *My tutor was quite **contemptuous** of my efforts.*

but:

> *Privately, even I had to agree that they really were **contemptible**.*

Militate means to have an influence against some evidence; **mitigate** means to reduce an effect, to soften or to appease:

> *The latest SAT results **militate** against the last inspection report.*

but:

> *The clarity and liveliness of Jeannie's story **mitigated** her general performance in school.*

Continuous means that something is without a break; **continual** means that something happens regularly:

> *On their way to the swimming baths, the class walked in a **continuous** line.*

but:

> *There is a **continual** outburst of delight every Friday.*

Different means that **this** is not like **that**; **differing** means that opinions or evidence clash:

> This year's Y6 class is quite **different** from last year's.

but:

> The staff sat in silence as the **differing** views of the head and her deputy thickened the air of the tiny staff room.

Allusion means a rather indirect reference to something that you probably know about; **illusion** means an idea that does not fit reality:

> Without mentioning any names or any events, the head made an **allusion** to the incident at the outdoor pursuits centre that lost the school its best speller.

but:

> The miscalculated test results caused us to live in a happy **illusion** until the SATs brought in reality.

Stationary means without movement; **stationery** means paper, pens, etc:

> Luckily, the class knew they had to be quite **stationary** before crossing a busy road.

but:

> We were distraught by the lack of paper until the **stationery** supplies arrived.

It helps to use a dictionary often, for spellings, for meanings – especially shades of meaning – and simply to get into the habit of using a valuable source of information. Other books, such as Bill Bryson's *Troublesome Words,* may also help.

Professional suitability and style

All native users of a language learn, from their earliest experiences of it, to match their style to their audience, to their own purpose in speaking or writing and to the topic being discussed. This test is about your ability to tell the difference between appropriate and inappropriate style. In particular, try to avoid these stylistic usages:

Non-parallelism in lists

When you write a list, look at the words you use to introduce the list. Each item in the list should follow grammatically from that introduction:

> In future planning, I should remember to:
> (a) to plan who should be in each group;
> (b) friendship groups.

should be:

> In future planning, I should remember to:
> (a) plan who should be in each group;
> (b) consider friendship groups.

No native user of English would say or write:

> *In future planning, I should remember to to plan who should be in each group.*

or:

> *In future planning, I should remember to friendship groups.*

Inconsistent register and tone

We can make a mistake with the tone of what we write. This is usually because we use a tone that is too formal or one that is too informal. Most writing is formal so a formal style is more appropriate in most cases.

An inconsistent style can show itself in the use of colloquialisms:

> *It was reported last night that the Secretary of State was **doing her nut** over the slow progress of her latest initiative for small rural schools.*

The opening phrase, *'It was reported,'* implies that the speaker was a newsreader and the intended audience the general public. *'Doing her nut'* is inappropriate in a news report. The tone and style should be appropriate to the audience.

This would be more consistent in tone if it was written like this:

> *It was reported last night that the Secretary of State was **concerned** over the slow progress of her latest initiative for small rural schools.*

An inconsistency of tone can also be created by mixing the use of active and passive constructions in the same sentence:

> *Some of the children **opened** [active] the letters for home, **read** [active] them and **were torn up** [passive].*

should be either:

> *Some of the children **opened** [active] the letters for home, **read** [active] them and **tore them up** [active].*

or:

> *Some of the letters for home **were opened** [passive] by the children, **read** [passive] and **torn up** [passive].*

In this last example, the auxiliary verb *were* has been left out from *were read* and *were torn up*. That is another case of *ellipsis*, what Dan Slobin calls *optional deletion*.

Finally, an inconsistent tone can also be created by mixing the use of the informal **you** and the more formal **one** in the same sentence. **You** is almost universal in speech, in sentences such as:

> *You never can tell.*

You is also appropriate in writing, especially informal writing; it is also appropriate in fairly formal writing. What is inappropriate is to mix the two styles:

> Since **you** played such an active role in last year's Easter Fair, **one** should take up the challenge again this year.

should be:

> Since **you** played such an active role in last year's Easter Fair, **you** should take up the challenge again this year.

On the other hand:

> Although **you** always found that the middle term used to be the most productive, **one** finds the level of production more evenly spread over the year now.

should be:

> Although **one** always found that the middle term used to be the most productive, **one** finds the level of production more evenly spread over the year now.

or:

> Although **I** always found that the middle term used to be the most productive, **I** find the level of production more evenly spread over the year now.

Both *one* and *you* can mean *people in general* or *people like us or me*. *You* can sometimes be confusing if it both carries that very general meaning and also means the other person. In other words, *you* is usually a second person pronoun, coming between *I* and *she/he/it*, and it can be confusing if it used as a third person pronoun like *one*.

Be consistent.

Shift in person within sentences or across sentences

This is related to the last point above. Like that, it is related to what happens when formal and informal styles or register get mixed. It is also related to *cohesion* and the use of pronouns. If you mean the same people, do not confuse things by referring to them as *you* when you really mean *they*:

> Too many **people** are leaving doors open when **you** shouldn't.

should be:

> Too many **people** are leaving doors open when **they** shouldn't.

or:

> Too many **of you** are leaving doors open when **you** shouldn't.

One hopes that the new community room will be ready before next term begins so that *we* can make full use of it.

should be:

We hope that the new community room will be ready before next term begins so that *we* can make full use of it.

Like many problems with writing, they can be reduced greatly if you get into and keep the habit of reading what you write as you write it, re-reading chunks and checking it at the end. Keep an eye on what you mean to say.

Excessive length and rambling sentences

This issue is related to earlier ones about abandoned constructions and failures to observe sentence boundaries. The key point is to see if very long sentences can be rewritten as more than one sentence. Long sentences are more than acceptable but only if the writer can control them:

Charlie is obviously a child that although has developed a high level of phonic understanding and is capable of breaking down unknown words is still with my regards to the definition of a reader not successful.

should be:

Charlie obviously has a high level of phonic understanding. He is able to break down unknown words. However, he is still not a successful reader in my view.

The uncorrected sentence above is a genuine product of a student-teacher. So is the following sentence:

With certain aspects of literacy I agree with Yetta Goodman (1980) whose research indicated that literacy is a naturally occurring and developing process in 'our literate society', however, this development is minimal in comparison with the expected requirements, for example children may naturally occur certain literacy skills.

should be:

Concerning certain aspects of literacy, I agree with Yetta Goodman (1980) whose research indicated that literacy is a naturally occurring and developing process in our literate society. This development is minimal in comparison with the expected requirements. For example, children may naturally acquire certain literacy skills.

You might have noticed that the uncorrected version has other problems, unconnected with sentence length or boundary. Problems rarely come singly.

Redundancy/tautology

If an expression means what you want to say, there is no need to add to it. It would make no sense to refer to the *QCA Authority* because the acronym means *Qualifications and Curriculum Authority*.

*The head reported that the governing body had **definitely** excluded Aloysius.*

should be:

The head reported that the governing body had excluded Aloysius.

Exclusion is itself a word with no limits so there is no point in saying that it is *definite*.

Some kinds of apparent redundancy are more problematic. One change in standard English over recent decades is that the verb *check* has almost been replaced by *check out*. They mean the same but it could be argued that the apparently redundant *out* is now part of a developing standard English.

Inappropriate conjunctions (also known as connectives)

Look at what was said above about relative pronouns and relative clauses in *Problems with relative pronouns in subordinate clauses*. Clauses that begin with *who, whom, which, that* are in a different category from those that begin with one of the long list of connectives such as *if, because, unless, so that, in case, although,* etc. All these words can begin a subordinate clause but the relationship with the main clause is different.

*The trouble with Roy is **because** he will not buckle down to hard work.*

should be:

*The trouble with Roy is **that** he will not buckle down to hard work.*

or:

*There is trouble with Roy **because** he will not buckle down to hard work.*

Some problems occur because the main clause has been completed and there seems to be a break in the writer's thinking before continuing with the subordinate clause:

*Roy's improvement has been **so** dramatic **so that** he could be quite near the top this year.*

should be:

*Roy's improvement has been dramatic **so** he could be quite near the top this year.*

or:

*Roy's improvement has been **so** dramatic **that** he could be quite near the top this year.*

Some conjunctions occur not only between clauses but also between phrases and even between single words. The problem is that sometimes these necessary words get left out:

The head received a long silence at the staff meeting when he announced his intention to sing dance at the interval during the Christmas play.

should be:

*The head received a long silence at the staff meeting when he announced his intention to sing **and** dance at the interval during the Christmas play.*

Remember that you will not be tested on all the items in this section nor is this list a syllabus. A glance at the sheer bulk of any grammar text should remind you that this is not exhaustive.

If you get stuck at any point, re-read what you have done, ask if it makes clear sense and see if it is as consistent with the rest of the sentence, paragraph or text as you can make it.

Questions

The actual test is computerised. You will be shown part of a sentence and then presented with a range of optional clauses or phrases that might complete the sentence. Decide which would be the best option to complete the sentence grammatically and drag it into the space provided. The test in this book involves you in precisely the same kind of thinking as the computerised test.

The grammar section of the test asks you to complete some sentences. That tests your ability to detect when something is wrong. You will see the first part of a sentence and then four optional ways to complete it. Three of these options are wrong or unsatisfactory in some way. Your task is to choose the best way to complete the sentence.

There are three tests of grammar:

- **of your ability to detect unrelated participles;**

- **of your ability to detect the wrong tense or tense inconsistency;**

- **of your ability to detect any lack of agreement between subject and verb.**

Unrelated participles

In the following tests, underline the one sentence that seems to you to be **appropriate in its use of a related participle rather than an unrelated one**:

TEST A

1. Realising the role that speech plays in helping children to solve practical tasks, it follows that children should be given tasks that require talk.

2. Realising the role that speech plays in helping children to solve practical tasks, Vygotsky placed language at the centre of all learning.

3. Realising the role that speech plays in helping children to solve practical tasks, language was seen by Vygotsky as central to learning.

4. Realising the role that speech plays in helping children to solve practical tasks, children's unassisted work is stressed by many teachers.

TEST B

1. Persuaded by her staff that afternoon playtimes were increasingly disruptive, the head decided to have no playtimes in the afternoon but to end school ten minutes early.

2. Persuaded by her staff that afternoon playtimes were increasingly disruptive, afternoon play was abandoned by the head and replaced with an earlier hometime.

3. Persuaded by her staff that afternoon playtimes were increasingly disruptive, the school exchanged its afternoon play for a shorter afternoon session.

4. Persuaded by her staff that afternoon playtimes were increasingly disruptive, the children had no play but could leave school ten minutes earlier.

TEST C

1. The curriculum, according to Peters, is not wholly an end in itself, conceding that even history can be viewed in an instrumental way.

2. Peters believes that the curriculum is not wholly an end in itself, conceding that even history can be viewed in an instrumental way.

3. Conceding that even history can be viewed in an instrumental way, the view that the curriculum is an end in itself is not fully supported by Peters.

4. Conceding that even history can be viewed in an instrumental way, Peters' view of the curriculum is not wholly in favour of education as an end in itself.

TEST D

1. Thought to be the easiest class in the school to teach, the head was surprised by the mayhem they caused during silent reading.

2. Thought to be the easiest class in the school to teach, it was surprising to the head that they could cause so much mayhem during silent reading.

3. Thought to be the easiest class in the school to teach, the mayhem they caused during silent reading was a surprise for the head.

4. Thought to be the easiest class in the school to teach, the children caused mayhem during silent reading.

Wrong tense or tense inconsistency

In the following tests, underline the one sentence that seems to you to be **appropriate in its use of the right and most consistent tense**:

TEST A

1. Although I wish now that I had worked harder, my degree result was very pleasing and it has meant being able to be more ambitious in the applications I made.

2. Although I wish now that I had worked harder, my degree result was very pleasing and it has meant that I have been able to be more ambitious in the applications I made.

3. Although I wish now that I had worked harder, my degree result was very pleasing and it has meant that I was able to be more ambitious in the applications I made.

4. Although I wish now that I had worked harder, my degree result was very pleasing and it has meant that I am able to be more ambitious in the applications I made.

TEST B

1. I don't consider myself a very gifted person, although I did well enough, but my headteacher father believes I'll make a good teacher and that, although I have always been a little naïve, life was good.

2. I don't consider myself a very gifted person, although I did well enough, but my headteacher father believes I'll make a good teacher and that, although I have always been a little naïve, life being good.

3. I don't consider myself a very gifted person, although I did well enough, but my headteacher father believes I'll make a good teacher and that, although I have always been a little naïve, life is good.

4. I don't consider myself a very gifted person, although I did well enough, but my headteacher father believes I'll make a good teacher and that, although I have always been a little naïve, life will be good.

TEST C

1. Whatever I do, my mind fills with thoughts of what could happen if I chose a school where I can't fit in, the children don't respond, the staff are cold and unhelpful and the head is bad-tempered.

2. Whatever I do, my mind fills with thoughts of what could happen if I chose a school where I can't fit in, the children won't respond, the staff are cold and unhelpful and the head was bad-tempered.

3. Whatever I do, my mind fills with thoughts of what could happen if I chose a school where I can't fit in, the children won't respond, the staff are cold and unhelpful and the head has been bad-tempered.

4. Whatever I do, my mind fills with thoughts of what could happen if I chose a school where I can't fit in, the children won't respond, the staff are cold and unhelpful and the head being bad-tempered.

TEST D

1. Perhaps the best action for me to take is to talk with friends, at least once I have examined what different areas offer, compared facilities, accommodation and opportunities and growing a little more sure of myself.

2. Perhaps the best action for me to take is to talk with friends, at least once I have examined what different areas offer, compared facilities, accommodation and opportunities and grow a little more sure of myself.

3. Perhaps the best action for me to take is to talk with friends, at least once I have examined what different areas offer, compared facilities, accommodation and opportunities and grew a little more sure of myself.

4. Perhaps the best action for me to take is to talk with friends, at least once I have examined what different areas offer, compared facilities, accommodation and opportunities and grown a little more sure of myself.

Lack of agreement between subject and verb

In the following tests, underline the one sentence that seems to you to be **appropriate in its agreement between subject and verb**:

TEST A

1. The trouble with both the way I talk and the way I write are that for much of the time I cannot trust myself to remember what I started with.

2. The trouble with both the way I talk and the way I write were that for much of the time I cannot trust myself to remember what I started with.

3. The trouble with both the way I talk and the way I write was that for much of the time I cannot trust myself to remember what I started with.

4. The trouble with both the way I talk and the way I write is that for much of the time I cannot trust myself to remember what I started with.

TEST B

1. A friend told me that the likeliest cause of this problem is that the unrelentingly abusive attitudes shown by my first English teacher is quite traumatic for me.

2. A friend told me that the likeliest cause of this problem is that the unrelentingly abusive attitudes shown by my first English teacher were quite traumatic for me.

3. A friend told me that the likeliest cause of this problem is that the unrelentingly abusive attitudes shown by my first English teacher was quite traumatic for me.

4. A friend told me that the likeliest cause of this problem is that the unrelentingly abusive attitudes shown by my first English teacher being quite traumatic for me.

TEST C

1. I wish it were that simple. In fact, are it that teacher, the one who helped me somehow to qualify for university, the sicknesses I had as a child or my supportive but rather stern parents?

2. I wish it were that simple. In fact, were it that teacher, the one who helped me somehow to qualify for university, the sicknesses I had as a child or my supportive but rather stern parents?

3. I wish it were that simple. In fact, was it that teacher, the one who helped me somehow to qualify for university, the sicknesses I had as a child or my supportive but rather stern parents?

4. I wish it were that simple. In fact, is it that teacher, the one who helped me somehow to qualify for university, the sicknesses I had as a child or my supportive but rather stern parents?

TEST D

1. Now that I am about to get a job, I know that the future, whether I am lucky or not or leave teaching or stay with it, and whatever anyone else does or says, was mine to make.

2. Now that I am about to get a job, I know that the future, whether I am lucky or not or leave teaching or stay with it, and whatever anyone else does or says, has been mine to make.

3. Now that I am about to get a job, I know that the future, whether I am lucky or not or leave teaching or stay with it, and whatever anyone else does or says, will be mine to make.

4. Now that I am about to get a job, I know that the future, whether I am lucky or not or leave teaching or stay with it, and whatever anyone else does or says, will have been mine to make.

4 | Comprehension

Introduction

8–12 marks are available for comprehension.

Most of the test is about writing. This section is about reading.

Teachers now have to read a great deal of written material about their professional lives and work. This material can be government documents (for example, on the law concerning exclusion from school), the educational press and very frequent information about the local educational scene. Because every teacher now has to do so much professionally demanding reading, there is a greater stress than there was previously on their being able to:

- **say what the main points of a text are;**
- **infer and deduce;**
- **tell fact from opinion;**
- **understand that some points made in a text are more important than others;**
- **present something of what they have read in a different way;**
- **retrieve factual information;**
- **adapt information read for a specific audience;**
- **re-assemble information that is distributed across a text;**
- **look for evidence about things in the text and judge, for example, if something is said implicitly or explicitly.**

The test will expect you to:

- **identify the key points in a text;**
- **read between the lines so that you make inferences and draw deductions;**
- **tell the difference between fact and fiction;**
- **understand that this point is more significant than that point and to know what that relative difference means for the text as a whole;**
- **read the text well enough to be able to present some of its content in a different way from the original;**
- **read a text and take from it particular items;**
- **put together material from different parts of the text;**
- **look for evidence in the text that confirms or disconfirms a statement about the text;**
- **make judgements; for example, is this point explicit or implicit in the text?**

The test you take will test only a selection of these aspects of literacy.

The comprehension test presents candidates with a short text and a series of questions on it. Read the whole text first. Good reading means paying almost simultaneous attention to the word or phrase you are concentrating on at the time and also to as much of the whole text as you have read and can keep in mind. To do this test well, you will need to focus on what is significant in the whole text so that you are able to select those bits and ignore the rest. Some questions ask you to see how this bit of the text relates to that bit, to notice how parts of the text are organised, to sequence ideas and to check what some phrases or words mean in the context. None of this is extraordinary and an attentive and reasonably experienced reader should not have difficulties.

Questions?

Read the following report, based on legislative changes, and then use the information you gain from it to complete the tasks and answer the questions that follow:

The Education of Young People in Care

The Children Act requires schools and their Local Authorities to provide for children who are 'Looked After' (that is, in Public Care). What does this mean for schools?

In an effort to improve the educational achievement of 'Looked After Children', the DCSF sees schools, Social Services and LAs as corporate parents with the responsibility collectively to care for them. To give them a chance to achieve what most children achieve, higher expectations than have been current must be set. This means ensuring their regular and sustained attendance, support for those with Special Educational Needs and, where appropriate, a clear policy regarding homework. All those involved in attending to the needs of Looked After Children must work harder to guarantee their equal opportunities. There are some, whether from ethnic minority groups or who are disabled, who have suffered from double discrimination.

At school level, this will all lead to some revision of policy documents regarding bullying, exclusion from school, Special Educational Needs and school behaviour. The child himself or herself will collaborate with the school and other concerned professionals in devising targets that will appear in a Personal Education Plan (PEP). Review meetings will be statutory: the child's teacher should attend, if possible, and a written report on the child's progress towards meeting the targets set will be presented. The PEP should also be reviewed at the same time and any outcome should be discussed with Social Services.

As there are no arrangements at the moment for schools to liaise with LAs and Social Services about these children, each school will have to appoint someone to act as a designated teacher, responsible for co-ordinating their support: maintaining swift communication with other concerned bodies, making sure that each child has a PEP and a Home–School Agreement and speaking for the child. This highly responsible job will require further training.

Since the aim of this new initiative is to make it possible for such children to approach or match the educational achievement of their peers, it is necessary for them to have full access to the National Curriculum or an equivalent flexible learning package. Although some will have Special Educational Needs, most should find that mainstream schools provide what they need, without their being statemented.

Ultimately, it is hoped that a persistent cycle of problems and difficulty can be broken by intervening powerfully through this initiative.

Attributing statements to categories

Read the statements below and decide which refer to:

DCSF	[DC]
LAs	[LA]
Looked After Children	[LC]
Schools	[Ss]

Put the right code in the box to the left of each statement. In the computerised test, you will be asked to drag the code to the box.

[ ]   They must appoint someone to speak for the 'Looked After Child'.

[ ]   It has given responsibility to corporate parents.

[ ]   They will need to check their policy statements.

[ ]   Their relationship with Social Services and schools will be closely linked.

[ ]   Most are expected to settle well in mainstream schools.

> **HINT**   Even this one question should tell you that comprehension demands careful judgement as well as knowledge. Don't rush.

Completing a bulleted list

Reread paragraphs 2–5. In the computerised test, you will be asked to select three phrases from a list and drag a tick symbol (✓) to boxes that show your chosen answers. Here, simply put an asterisk by the three that are appropriate. One has been identified for you.

In future, the 'Looked After Child':

- **will be expected to attend school more regularly**

[ ]   will not suffer from discrimination.

[ ]   will work in a mainstream school.

[ ]   will match the educational achievement of their peers.

[ ]   will have a designated teacher.

[ ]   may have to work harder.

[ ]   will have a flexible learning package.

[ ]   will be able to attend Review Meetings.

[ ]   will work with others responsible to devise targets.

[ ]   will be expected to attend school more regularly.

Sequencing information

From the seven statements below, select the four that most informatively and accurately reflect the four major stages of the initiative. You should follow the sequence set out in the passage. Put *1, 2, 3* or *4* in the appropriate box. In the computerised test, you will be asked to drag the words *FIRST, SECOND, THIRD* and *FOURTH* to boxes beside your answers.

[ ] School policies to be revised accordingly.

[ ] A homework policy to be set up.

[ ] A designated teacher to be appointed.

[ ] The SENCO should be involved.

[ ] Schools, Social Services and LAs to be established as corporate parents.

[ ] A PEP to be drawn up.

[ ] The LEA should liaise with schools.

Presenting main points

From the list of eight statements below, select the five that most accurately say what should happen to promote the education of 'Looked After Children'. Put an asterisk in the box by each of your chosen five. In the computerised test, you will be asked to drag the tick symbol to show your choices.

[ ] The child's teacher should attend the Review Meeting.

[ ] Higher expectations than hitherto must be set.

[ ] Schools' policies must be in line with their new responsibility.

[ ] The Special Needs consultant must be involved.

[ ] A designated teacher must be appointed.

[ ] A PEP must be drawn up.

[ ] The School Behaviour Policy will have to be redrawn.

[ ] Schools, Social Services and LAs should be *corporate parents* for these children.

Matching texts to summaries

From the list of four statements below, select the one that most effectively summarises paragraphs 3–5 and put an asterisk in the box beside it. In the computerised test, you will be asked to drag a tick symbol to a box beside your chosen answer.

[ ] Policies and policy documents will have to be revised to take account of the 'Looked After Child'.

[ ] The school and its designated teacher will be responsible for helping 'Looked After Children' to achieve educationally at a level close to their peers.

[ ] The PEP will ensure that the educational needs of the 'Looked After Children' are catered for.

[ ] The designated teacher will be crucial to the success of this initiative.

Identifying the meaning of words and phrases

From each list of five statements below, select and mark the one that most reflects the meaning of the quoted statement. Put an asterisk in the appropriate box. In the computerised test, you will be asked to drag a tick symbol to your answer.

'higher expectations than have been current must be set' (para 2) is nearest in meaning to:

[ ] there must be more homework for 'Looked After Children';

[ ] the school must expect attendance and provide for appropriate support and work;

[ ] the schools' policies must be revised to promote the education of 'Looked After Children';

[ ] the child must attend school on a more regular basis than previously;

[ ] the corporate parents must ensure equal opportunities for 'Looked After Children'.

'Review meetings will be statutory' (para 3) is nearest in meaning to:

[ ] a meeting will be held to write a report on the 'Looked After Child';

[ ] a meeting must be held that will review the progress of the PEP;

[ ] a meeting will be held where the designated teacher reviews progress;

[ ] a meeting will be held so that Social Services are kept informed;

[ ] a meeting will be held where the child's teacher can review its progress.

Evaluating statements about the text

Read each of the statements about the 'Looked After Child' Initiative and decide which of them:

- is *supported* by the text [*S*];
- is either *implied* to be the case or is implicitly supported by the text [*I*];
- says something for which there is *no evidence* or information in the text [NE];
- is *implicitly contradicted* or refuted by the text [*IC*];
- is *explicitly contradicted* or refuted by the text [*C*].

Put the appropriate code in each box. In the computerised test, you will be asked to drag the code to its box.

[ ] The Looked After Child's teacher will become the designated teacher.

[ ] Schools should use existing arrangements for liaison with Social Services and LAs.

[ ] The corporate parents will need to ensure equal opportunities for 'Looked After Children' with muscular dystrophy.

[ ] The school attendance record of 'Looked After Children' needs to be maintained.

[ ] The initiative aims to stop the cyclical pattern of problems for these children.

[ ] 'Looked After Children' have special needs.

[ ] The designated teacher will talk with Social Services after the Review meeting.

Selecting headings and sub-headings

From the list of four statements below, select the one that would be the most appropriate sub-heading to appear just above the second paragraph. Put an asterisk in the box by your choice. In the computerised test, you will be asked to drag a tick to the box.

[ ] Corporate parents and their role.

[ ] The needs of 'Looked After Children'.

[ ] The issue of equal opportunities.

[ ] The responsibilities of the LA.

Identifying the audience

From the list of five possible audiences for this text, given below, select the one that you think would be **M**ost relevant and put the code **M** in the appropriate box. Put **L** beside the audience for whom the passage would be **L**east relevant. In the computerised test, you will be asked to drag and drop the letter **M** into the box next to the statement you consider **M**ost relevant and the **L** into the box next to the statement you consider to be **L**east relevant.

[ ] Parents of 'Looked After Children'.

[ ] 'Looked After Children'.

[ ] Headteachers and their governors.

[ ] Those about to qualify as teachers.

[ ] Designated teachers.

5 | Answers and key points

Spelling

1. *independent*

   Key point
   Most words that end with that sound end in *-ent*.

2. *demonstrable*

   Key point
   Some words, like **demonstrate**, **educate**, lose an element when they gain a suffix.

3. *assessment*

   Key point
   Words vary in the way that they spell the **s** sound. This word has two pairs of double **s**.

4. *adolescents*

   Key point
   Words vary in the way they spell the **s** sound. This word uses **sc.**

5. *pursue*

   Key point
   The sound represented here by **ur** is represented by different letter-strings in other words. They simply have to be learned by heart.

6. stories

   Key point
   Luckily, this is one of the most reliable rules. Nouns that end in a consonant and *-y,* such as **fairy, party**, etc, drop the **y** and add *-ies* in the plural form.

7. *weighing*

   Key point
   This is clear but complex. If the sound is **ee**, the rule for using **i** and **e** together really is '**ie** except after **c**'. If the sound is not **ee**, the **e** comes first.

8. *fuelled*

   Key point
   Verbs that end in a single *-l*, like **instil**, take a second **l** when either *-ed* or *-ing* is added.

9. *affect*

   Key point
   The distinction between **affect** and **effect** baffles many educated adults. If you **affect** something, you have an **effect** on it. Try that as a mnemonic, with the **a** of **affect** coming first, as in the alphabet.

10. *responsibility*

> **Key point**
> Another case of having to learn by heart. There are just two ways to spell the suffixes we find in **capable** and **terrible**. Of **-able/ible** and **ability/ibility**, **able/ability** is the more common.

11. *practice*

> **Key point**
> Practice/practise and advice/advise confuse a lot of us. The words ending in **-ice** are nouns and could have the word **the** before them; the words ending in **-ise** are verbs and could have the word **I** in front of them.

12. *disappear*

> **Key point**
> Morphology, the way that words are built up from their parts, helps here. The prefixes **mis-** and **dis-** end in a single **-s**. What follows is a stem word, like **-take** or **-appear**. Those who write **dissappear** have imagined a non-existent prefix **diss-**.

13. *possesses*

> **Key point**
> Here, the sound **s** is represented twice by **ss**. The double **ss** is very likely in the middle of a word and quite likely at the end.

14. *impracticability*

> **Key point**
> This is a mixture of morphology and the need to learn by heart whether a word uses -**able** or **-ible**. The morphology involved is a series of prefix + stem + suffix + suffix: **im + practice + able + ity**. **Practice** loses **e**; **able** changes.

15. *rigorous*

> **Key point**
> The stem word, the abstract noun **rigour**, drops the **u** when it adds the adjective suffix **-ous.** This happens in other words, such as **labour, laborious** (but notice the added **i** in **laborious**).

16. *exaggerate*

> **Key point**
> Remember that the commonest type of misspelling is the use or non-use of the double consonant (incidentally, notice that word **misspelling**.) This is one of the hardest to remember because there are no analogies.

17. *regrettably*

> **Key point**
> This is not about **able/ible** but about the way that a verb that ends in a consonant such as **t** is likely to double that consonant when an adverb suffix, such as **-ably**, is added. There are also analogies with **forget, forgettably**.

18. *automatic*

> **Key point**
> Apart from the use of a Greek suffix, **auto-**, meaning **self**, it is also a case of a fairly long and complex word whose spelling is close to the way it is said.

19. *petition*

> **Key point**
> Another example of the use of the suffix **-tion**. There are several ways to spell this sound, from **ocean** to **suspicion**, so which it is needs to be learned.

20. *gaffe*

> **Key point**
> Foreign words are inevitably a problem because they use different letter-strings from English and are consequently harder to predict. Learn them by heart after studying them very carefully.

21. *fifth*

> **Key point**
> Several ordinal numbers – for example, **sixth, eighth** – have an unusual collection of consonants at the end of the word and need to be studied and learned by heart.

22. *allowed*

> **Key point**
> There has been a great increase in confusion between **allowed/a loud/aloud, allot/a lot**, etc.; it is serious because it shows that the writer does very little reading and that the simple grammatical and meaning distinctions between the participle **allowed** and the adverb **aloud** have been overlooked.

23. *supersede*

> **Key point**
> This is one of the few words to represent that final sound with **-sede**. Analogies with **concede, succeed** do not work but more familiarity and learning by heart do.

24. *maturity*

> **Key point**
> It is another example of the way that an adjective, **mature,** drops the final **e** when the noun suffix **-ity** is added but it is also quite regular phonically.

25. *medicinal*

> **Key point**
> Some words retain elements of their original stem word (**medicine**), despite some changes in the sounds spoken, so that the related meanings can be preserved.

Punctuation

1. *As soon as we speak, (1) we reveal a great deal of ourselves to our audience. Suppose you ask someone,*

   (2) 'Shall we have a drink? (3)' (4)

   Suppose the other person replies, (5)

   'Yes, I'd like a whiskey, (6) me.'

   That tag, *me*, tells you that the speaker probably comes from (7) Manchester.

   Sometimes, what people say does tell you something about their origin but it is less definite. A friend asks you and another friend,

   'Now, what would youse two like to drink?'

   The questioner may or may not come from Ireland but will certainly have a background there because that use of (8) 'youse', unknown in standard English, has its roots in the Irish having one form of 'you' for one person (9) (tú) and another form of 'you' for two people (9) (sibh). Of course, none of this means that any of these speakers could speak any Irish! (10)

   ### Key points

   (1) The subordinate clause appears first so it should be separated from the main clause by a comma.

   (2) The first letter in the sentence needs a capital letter.

   (3) A question requires a question mark.

   (4) Direct speech needs speech marks both at the beginning and at the end. The two marks, paired, form a consistency.

   (5) The mark before a direct quotation is usually a comma.

   (6) A comma is needed to separate the tag 'me' from the rest.

   (7) The city of Manchester requires a capital letter.

   (8) This is a bit of language that differs from the rest of the text and needs quotation marks to identify it.

   (9) The Irish words tú and sibh break into the rest and are best placed within brackets.

   (10) This is a mild exclamation but an exclamation it is. It needs the exclamation mark.

2. *If we look at boys' (11) performance in English, we have to agree that there is, generally, (12) some cause for concern. Is there anything that can be done to help them to improve?*

   Among the approaches that seemed to help boys in their reading are: (13)

   enthusiastically-(14)encouraged private reading;
   clearly-set tasks; (15)
   explicit teaching of reading strategies;

a wide range of outcomes from reading;
reading preferences that are discussed.

The (16) DfEE's anxiety was evident in the QCA report (17) 'Can Do Better.' However, (18) its analysis of the situation was coupled with extremely supportive case studies that suggest helpful (19) short-term plans and long-term strategies.

Key points

(11) The performance belongs to the boys so an apostrophe is needed after the **s.**

(12) The interruption of the flow of the sentence by the word **generally** should be marked by twinned commas, one before and one after the word.

(13) A list is being introduced so a colon is needed.

(14) A hyphen should link the two words to make one word. The example on the following line shows what to be consistent with.

(15) Each item in this list is more than one word long and needs a semicolon to separate each item from the next.

(16) The Department for Education and Employment, conventionally, uses a set of three capitals for the content words and a lower case for the preposition.

(17) The title of a document should be in single quotation marks.

(18) After the introductory sentence adverb **However**, interrupting the flow of the sentence, a comma is needed.

(19) The plan is not in the short term but short-term; before the noun, and treated as one word, it should be hyphenated.

---

3. *What is it about (20) standard English that makes it standard? (21)*

    (22)
    Like every language, English has gone through many changes. The Saxons and Angles who settled here brought their own languages with them, (23) predominantly Saxon, and after a while the dialects of Anglo-Saxon overcame the Celtic languages that had flourished along with Latin until soon after the Romans left in 410AD. The languages spoken by the later Scandinavian invaders were probably just about intelligible to some of the Anglo-(24)Saxons but changes and borrowings continued: the new invaders' (25) legacy to us includes **they**, **them**, **their**. Anglo-Saxon, modified by Scandinavian, with dialects that were barely intelligible to other Anglo-Saxon speakers, continued for hundreds of years but, thankfully, (26) it became simpler. (27) The German word for **big** is **gross** but it has six versions. Our Anglo-Saxon ancestors had eleven versions of adjectives; (28) we have just three: **big, bigger, biggest.** Even when we complicate matters by having **good, better,** (29) **best,** that is still easier than Anglo-Saxon! (30)

Key Points

(20) There is no need for a capital for **standard**; the lower case version is now the accepted convention.

(21) A question requires a question mark.

(22) After the first sentence, comes the beginning of an answer. A new paragraph is needed.

(23) **predominantly Saxon** breaks into the sentence and needs a pair of commas, one before and one after.

(24) A hyphen is needed for Anglo-Saxon (as for Irish-American).

(25) The noun is **invaders** so they need an apostrophe before **legacy**.

(26) **Thankfully** is also an interruption and a pair of commas is needed.

(27) A sentence ends with a full stop.

(28) There are two sentences but their meanings are so closely related that they need a semi-colon to link them.

(29) The series of three items in a list without an **and** requires a series of commas.

(30) This is an exclamation but that shows how personal punctuation is.

Grammar

Unrelated participles

A 2 *Vygotsky* is the one who did the *realising*; who *realised*.
B 1 The *head* was the one who was *persuaded*.
C 2 It was *Peters* who *conceded*, who did the *conceding*, not his views.
D 4 The *children were thought*, nobody and nothing else.

> **Key point**
> This relates to the issue of agreement between subject and verb. You clarify the matter by asking **who did** it.

Wrong tense or tense consistency

A 2

> **Key point**
> **have been** makes most sense because it matches or agrees with the other verbs: the series of **wish** and **had worked** followed by **was** and **has meant**. **Made** confirms the choice of **have been** because it makes **was** impossible.

B 4

> **Key point**
> When there are several verbs in a sentence, some in different tenses, the question is to decide what other verb this one should be like. This verb is part of a series beginning *I'll make* and so is in the future tense.

C 1

Key point
There is a series of short clauses beginning with *I can't* and all have to use the same verb form.

D 4

Key point
grown makes most sense because it is the only option that fits the use of the verb form *have examined: compared* parallels *grown* because the two verbs make use of the *have* of *have examined.*

Lack of agreement between subject and verb

A 4

Key point
The subject of the sentence is *trouble,* a singular noun, so the verb has to be singular also: *is.* There can often be a problem with subjects whose headwords are a long way from the verb; it is very easy to be trapped into picking up the nearest noun and thinking that that is the subject (in this sentence, the trap is *way*). This question does also ask you to be careful about the tense: the present.

B 2

Key point
The subject is *attitudes* so the verb has to be in the plural: *were.* Again, there is always a problem with a sentence with several nouns: out of *friend, cause, problem, attitudes, teacher,* which is the subject of this verb? The correct tense confirms the answer.

C 3

Key point
This seems quite easy but the issue is that there are, apparently, several subjects: *teacher, illnesses, parents.* The clue is the word *or* which tells you, logically, that only one thing is the subject, not everything listed. This is confirmed by the singular *it.*

D 3

Key point
This time, the tense not only fits the grammar but also the obvious sense of *the future.*

Comprehension

Attributing statements to categories

[Ss] They must appoint someone to speak for the 'Looked After Child'.

> **Key point**
> Para 4 says that the schools must appoint a designated teacher whose responsibilities include *speaking for the child*.

[DC] It has given responsibility to corporate parents.

> **Key point**
> Para 2 says that *the DCSF sees schools, Social Services and LAs as corporate parents.*

[Ss] They will need to check their policy statements.

> **Key point**
> Para 3 says that *At school level ... some revision of policy documents.*

[LA] Their relationship with Social Services and schools will be closely linked.

> **Key point**
> Para 2 opens by saying that they will be *corporate parents.*

[LC] Most are expected to settle well in mainstream schools.

> **Key point**
> Para 5 says that *most should find that mainstream schools provide what they need.*

Completing a bulleted list

- **Will have a designated teacher.**

> **Key point**
> Para 4 says that schools will appoint a *designated teacher* to look after the interests of 'Looked After Children'.

- **Will work with others responsible to devise targets.**

> **Key point**
> Para 3 says that *the child itself will collaborate.*

- **May have to work harder.**

Key point
Para 2 says that *higher expectations than have been current must be set.* The children's work is implicit in this statement.

- **Will be expected to attend school more regularly.**

Key point
Para 2 says that *regular and sustained attendance* is a key feature of the higher expectations.

Sequencing information

[1] Schools, Social Services and LAs to be established as corporate parents.

Key point
This is a prerequisite of the rest.

[2] School policies to be revised accordingly.

Key point
Revising the policies and the documentation follows the DCSF decision; it is the first thing mentioned in Para 3.

[3] A PEP to be drawn up.

Key point
The PEP follows from the revised policies, as in the second sentence of Para 3.

[4] A designated teacher to be appointed.

Key point
This appointment arises from the need to have someone to have oversight of the PEP and to liaise with the LA and Social Services.

Presenting main points

[*] Higher expectations than hitherto must be set.

Key point
This demand is placed on all concerned; the other points flow from it.

[*] Schools' policies must be in line with their new responsibility.

Key point
This is how the school prepares itself for the enlarged responsibility.

[*] A designated teacher must be appointed.

Key point
This is a specific acting out of a key feature of the policy.

[*] A PEP must be drawn up.

Key point
This is how the policy is made right for the child.

[*] Schools, Social Services and LAs should be **corporate parents** for these children.

Key point
This is how the whole endeavour is ensured and monitored.

However, these points are not to be included:

The child's teacher should attend the Review Meeting.

Key point
This is preferable but not essential.

The special needs consultant must be involved.

Key point
This is not said anywhere although it remains a possibility.

The School Behaviour Policy will have to be redrawn.

Key point
Policy documents have to be checked and **may** – not will – have to be redrawn; behaviour is included among other documents

Matching texts to summaries

[ ] Policies and policy documents will have to be revised to take account of the 'Looked after Child'.

Key point
This will probably be necessary but it deals with only one factor out of several. **Do not choose this.**

[*] The school and its designated teacher will be responsible for helping 'Looked After Children' to achieve educationally at a level close to their peers'.

Key point
This is the only summary that answers the question: what is the role of the school? It is full, covering the main features, and also specific about functions and aims. *Choose this*.

[ ] The Personal Education Plan will ensure that the educational needs of the 'Looked After Children' are catered for.

Key point
That is its aim but the school and its staff are not mentioned, nor are its aims. *Do not choose this.*

[ ] The designated teacher will be crucial to the success of this initiative.

Key point
This is true but it ignores other key factors. *Do not choose this.*

Identifying the meaning of words and phrases

'higher expectations than have been current must be set' (para 2) is nearest in meaning to:

[ ] There must be more homework for 'Looked After Children'.

Key point
This is not what the passage says and ignores the range of expectations. *Do not choose it.*

[*] The school must expect attendance and provide for appropriate support and work.

Key point
This covers the range of expectations and fits the context of the passage. *Choose it.*

[ ] The schools' policies must be revised to promote the education of 'Looked After Children'.

Key point
This may be necessary but the expectations say more. *Do not choose it.*

[ ] The child must attend school on a more regular basis than previously.

Key point
This might be the case but it is not inevitably so and ignores other expectations. *Do not choose it.*

[ ] The corporate parents must ensure equal opportunities for 'Looked After Children'.

Key point
This is implicit rather than explicit and ignores other expectations. **Do not choose it.**

'Review meetings will be statutory' (para 3) is nearest in meaning to:

[ ] A meeting will be held to write a report on the 'Looked After Child'.

Key point
The report will be **presented** at the meeting, not written. **Do not choose it.**

[*] A meeting must be held that will review the progress of the PEP.

Key point
Must carries the meaning of **statutory** here. It follows the mention of the plan; reviewing that plan will meet the needs fully. **Choose this.**

[ ] A meeting will be held where the designated teacher reviews progress.

Key point
This may be so but it is not stated and other things are. **Do not choose it.**

[ ] A meeting will be held so that Social Services are kept informed.

Key point
This should result from the meeting but is not its real focus. **Do not choose it.**

[ ] A meeting will be held where the child's teacher can review its progress.

Key point
The teacher attends **if possible. Do not choose it.**

Evaluating statements about the text

[NE] The 'Looked After Child's' teacher will become the designated teacher.

Key point
This is not said anywhere.

[C] Schools should use existing arrangements for liaison with Social Services and LAs.

Key point
Para 4 says that there are no such arrangements at the moment.

[I] The corporate parents will need to ensure equal opportunities for 'Looked After Children' with muscular dystrophy.

Key point
The explicit reference to (any) disabled children has to imply those with muscular dystrophy, among others.

[IC] The school attendance record of 'Looked After Children' needs to be maintained.

Key point
There may be a need to improve their attendance; implicitly, it has to be *more than* maintained.

[S] The initiative aims to stop the cyclical pattern of problems for these children.

Key point
The final sentence says as much.

[C] 'Looked After Children' have special needs.

Key point
Ask: is this true of all, some or none? It claims to be generally true, true about all 'Looked After Children'. Para 2 says that there may be some.

[I] The designated teacher will talk with Social Services after the Review meeting.

Key point
Since it is part of the designated teacher's function to *communicate* with 'other bodies' and to *speak* for the child, it is implied that that s/he will talk with Social Services.

Selecting headings and sub-headings

[*] Corporate parents and their role.

Key point
This covers schools, LAs and Social Services and says that what follows will be about what they have to do. *Choose this.*

[ ] The needs of 'Looked After Children'.

Key point
This is what lies behind the passage but not what it deals with. *Do not choose it.*

[ ] The issue of equal opportunities.

Key point
This is just one factor out of several that are significant. *Do not choose it.*

[ ] The responsibilities of the LA.

Key point
They are included and implicit in what follows but the other bodies are ignored. ***Do not choose it.***

Identifying the audience

[ ] Parents of 'Looked After Children'.

Key point
These parents might be interested but 'Looked After Children' do not live with their biological parents. It is clearly directed at those who have day-to-day responsibility. ***Do not choose it.***

[L] 'Looked After Children'.

Key point
The language and tone of the passage is clearly not for children, even those so crucially involved. Their close connection with its outcomes does not mean that it is aimed at them. ***Do not choose it.***

[M] Headteachers and their governors.

Key point
The people who have the responsibility for making this initiative work in schools are, first, the head and, formally, the governors. ***Choose this.*** [M]

[ ] Those about to qualify as teachers.

Key point
They should be interested but not in the specific details given here. ***Choose it.*** [L]

[ ] Designated teachers.

Key point
They should be very interested indeed but probably in some document that more specifically addresses what they have to do. ***Do not choose it.***

Further reading

Bryson, B. (1986) *Troublesome Words*. Harmondsworth: Penguin Books.

Crystal, D. (2004) *Rediscover Grammar*. Harlow: Longman.

DfES (2000) *Grammar for Writing*. London: DCSF Publications Centre.

Greenbaum, S. (1996) *The Oxford English Grammar*. Oxford: OUP.

Medwell, J. et al. (2007) *Primary English – Knowledge and Understanding*, 3rd edition. Exeter: Learning Matters.

Trask, R. L. (1997) *The Penguin Guide to Punctuation*. Harmondsworth: Penguin Books.

Truss, L. (2003) *Eats, Shoots & Leaves*. London: Profile Books.

Glossary

*Abbreviation A shortened form of a word or phrase; usually, but not always, consisting of a letter or group of letters taken from the word or phrase. For example, the word *approximately* can be replaced by the abbreviation 'approx'.

*Acronym An abbreviation made from the initial letters of a group of words and often pronounced as a single word, for example, RAM (random access memory).

Accent An accent is the distinctive system of pronunciation that listeners identify as being used by a regional or social group. Accents are neither easy nor hard to follow, merely familiar or unfamiliar.

Adjective An adjective is a word, phrase or clause that tells us about a noun: **clever** *child*, **tense** *student*, **concerned** *teacher*; *a lesson **about Spain**; the teacher **who had done supply work there previously**.* The clause comes after the noun whereas the phrase may come before (*the **predictably over-anxious** child **from Ashton***) as well as more typically, afterwards.

Adverb Adverbs tell us when, where or how something took place. They usually modify verbs but can also modify adjectives, other adverbs or sentences: *Joe sang **happily**; Annie is a **very** engaged reader; Alice danced **very** gracefully; Lucy had, **fortunately**, brought her trumpet with her.*

Not all adverbs end in *ly. Fast* is usually used as an adverb. *Very,* used above, is an adverb that appears only as an intensifier of some other word.

Adverbial clause An adverbial clause does the work of an adverb: it tells us when, where or how something took place: *The head came into the hall **when all the children were there**; Ann did her print-making **where she usually worked**; Pam ran down the corridor **as if she was being chased**.*

Adverbial phrase An adverbial phrase also does the work of an adverb. It is a group of words based on an adverb but coming before or after it or both: **very quickly**, *talked **as volubly as** the deputy.* An adverb can be substituted for an adverbial phrase.

Agree/agreement If one person does something, the verb should be in its singular form: *Annie **sings**.* If more than one does something, the verb should be in its plural form: *Joe and Sally **are painting**.*

*Analogy Drawing a comparison to show a similarity; for example, if you were describing the flow of electricity, you might choose to use the flow of water as an analogy.

*Apostrophe A **punctuation mark** used for two purposes:

    – to show that something belongs to someone (the **possessive** form); for example, *the **pupil's** work,* or

    – to show that letters have been missed out (a **contraction**); for example, **you've** is the shortened form of *you have.*

Attachment ambiguity Ambiguity may arise when it is unclear if a phrase should be attached to this or that other phrase. In *The teacher told the class what had happened to the caretaker on the stairs,* it is possible to understand that *on the stairs* was where something happened to the caretaker but also that it was *on the stairs* that the teacher told the class.

*Audio Of, or relating to, sound.

Clause A group of words with a finite verb (it would be a phrase if it did not have a finite verb). As it is finite, the verb typically has a subject. A clause may be a sentence: *Alice*

laughed. A sentence may contain several clauses: *Alice laughed and Lucy giggled* links two clauses of equal significance with the conjunction *and*; this is a co-ordinate sentence. *Alice laughed because Lucy giggled* links two clauses that differ in significance; this is a complex sentence in which a main clause – *Alice laughed* – is linked to a subordinate clause that is not independent of other clauses but exists to explain the main clause on which it depends.

Coherence/cohesion A well-made text feels coherent. What holds it together is the writer's use of cohesion: cohesive devices that relate parts of the text to each other. Adverbs between sentences are such devices: *The IT suite was heavily used.* **However**, *rising numbers were putting pressure on its use.*

Repetition of a word or some reference to it is another device. Perhaps the one we are most aware of is the use of a pronoun to refer to its noun. A noun may refer back to its noun: *The Ofsted report was scrutinised by the Governors before* **it** *was presented to parents. Although* **some** *were apprehensive, most of the class looked forward to the cliff-walk.*

*Colloquial A colloquialism is a term used in everyday language rather than in formal speech or writing; for example, the use of the word *kids* rather than *children* in the following sentence:

The kids in Years 4 and 5 are having a swimming gala next week.

*Colon: see **punctuation.**

*Comma: see **punctuation.**

*Compound word A word made when two words are joined to form a new word; for example, *foot/ball, foot/fall.* Sometimes, a hyphen is used between the two parts of the word, as in *over-anxious.*

*Conjunctions (see also connectives) These are words such as *and*, *but* and *or*, that are used to join words, phrases or clauses. There are two kinds of conjunction:

- **Co-ordinating conjunctions** (*and*, *but*, *or* and *so*). These link items that have equal status grammatically, for example:
  We could fly to Paris **or** we could take the train.
  He plans to fly to Dublin **but** he will arrive there very early.

- **Subordinating conjunctions** (*when*, *while*, *before*, *after*, *since*, *until*, *if*, *because*, *although*, *that*). If the two items do not have equal status, a subordinating conjunction is used. Most commonly, this happens when a main clause is joined to a subordinate clause, for example:
  I was late for the meeting **because** the train was delayed.

Connective Connectives connect words, phrases, clauses and sentences. Those that operate *within* the sentence, that connect words, phrases and clauses, are called conjunctions: *and, but, if, or, because, although, etc.* Those that connect sentences (*Pam and Tom worked very hard all term.* **Luckily**, *their efforts paid off*) include some conjunctions but also adverbs such as: *On the other hand, Later, While we were singing, etc.*

Consistency A good style is, among other things, consistent. The writer will always spell *judgement* with that first *e* or always without it. Punctuation demands a very consistent style, as when adverbs such as *however* always appear between commas if they occur in the middle of a sentence.

*Consonant Consonants are letters and speech sounds that are not vowels. See **vowel.**

Contraction If we try to write down informal speech, we will sometimes need contractions. These help us to write some contracted combinations of words: *do not* becomes *don't*, *will not* becomes *won't*. The words are contracted by omitting some letters and inserting an apostrophe into the space that is left. Occasionally, as with *won't*, there is also a change in spelling.

*Contradict, contradicted, contradiction To contradict is to state that something is the opposite of what has been said; a contradiction is a statement that contradicts.

Convention While the rules of grammar, like the laws of gravity, get their authority by describing how things are, there are some practices that are matters of social convention and have no other explanation. The conventions governing spelling and punctuation, for example, have changed over time.

*Definite article The; see **determiner**.

*Determiner These are words used with nouns to help define them, for example, *this* *computer*, *a pencil*, *the book* and limit, i.e. determine the reference of the noun in some way. Determiners include:

- articles (*a/an, the*)
- demonstratives (*this/that, these/those*)
- possessives (*my/your/his/her/its/our/their*)
- quantifiers (*some, any, no, many, few, all, either, each*, etc.)
- numbers (*one, two, three*, etc.), and
- some question words (*which, what, whose*).

Words that are used as determiners are followed by a noun (though not necessarily immediately). For example, *this book is yours*; *this black book is yours*; *which book is yours?*

Many determiners can also be used as **pronouns.** These include demonstrative pronouns, question words, numbers and most quantifiers. When used as pronouns, determiners are not followed by a noun; they refer to the noun: **this** is for you (where *this* refers to *this school, this book*, etc.).

Dialect A variety of a language that is spoken by a specific group or in a specific area of the country and whose words and grammar show some differences from those used in other dialects of English. The prestige of a dialect derives from the prestige of its speakers, not from its linguistic features. *Accent* is usually taken to be related but different because it focuses on the *substance* of the language: in the case of an accent, that substance is the sound of speech.

*Dialogue A conversation between two or more people.

Digraph Two letters that represent one sound: *ch* and *ck* in *check*; *sh* in *show*; *ph* in *phonically*.

*Discourse marker A word or phrase (such as *however, nevertheless, well, OK*, or *right!*) that is used to signal a pause or change of direction in conversation.

Ellipsis If a sentence can be understood when a word or a group of words is removed, the parts deleted have been ellipted. One of the commonest examples of ellipsis is the dropping of the relative pronoun *that*: *The school* [**that**] *I like best*. A more sophisticated usage is: *My class, **if lively**, is still well-behaved*. *If lively* here is an ellipted version of something like *even if it is lively*.

*Evaluate To assess; when asked to evaluate whether a statement is supported or implied by a text, you are being asked to judge how clearly the text does or does not spell out the information given in the statement.

Grammar Grammar, or syntax, is usually used to mean how sentences are organised. It can, however, also refer to the organisation of larger units: the text level. *Cohesion* is the study of the grammar of these larger units. *Morphology* is the branch of grammar that deals with word-formation.

*Imply, implied, implicit Something implied is hinted at without being stated explicitly. It is implicit.

*Indefinite article *A* or *an*; see **determiner**.

Infinitive The (non-finite) form of a verb that opens with *to*: *to learn, to study, to think.*

Morpheme The smallest bit of language that has meaning. A morpheme may be a whole word (*cabbage*) or a word may have several morphemes (*un+help+ful, govern+or, head+teach+er.*) **Suffixes** and **prefixes** are all morphemes.

Morphology: see **grammar**.

Noun Nouns refer to objects, ideas, things, places. They take a plural form (usually, add *s*). Some nouns, however, do not normally take a plural form: *happiness.* They have a possessive form (add *'s* or *s'*). They can be substituted by a pronoun, take a word like *the, this, a* before them and take a verb after them.

- **Noun phrase**: a group of words that works as a noun. A pronoun could be substituted for it: *The first person to have been Chair of the Education Committee.*

- **Noun clause**: a group of words that has a finite verb and that acts as a noun. Here, the clause acts as the subject: ***That I was late with my reports yet again*** was hard to swallow. Here, it acts as the object: *The class was desperate to know **if the school trip was still on.***

- **Collective nouns** refer to a group of things or people: *collection, family, group, class, set.* It is usually safest to treat collective nouns as singular unless the meaning is that they should be read as plural.

- **Proper nouns** refer to specific people, places, organisations, etc, and have a capital initial letter: *Dot, Mike*; *Salford, Canterbury*; *Training and Development Agency.*

Paragraph One or more sentences grouped together because they are about the same topic or because they form one utterance in a dialogue. It is separated from the adjacent paragraphs by beginning on a new line.

Parenthesis A word or phrase that interrupts the sentence is marked at both boundaries by parentheses: brackets, commas or dashes:

The Irwell (which flows through Salford) was the focus of their local studies.

The Irwell – which flows through Salford – was the focus of their local studies.

The Irwell, which flows through Salford, was the focus of their local studies.

Participle The present participle is a form of the verb that ends in *ing*: *learning, reading, writing*; the past participle is a form of the verb that ends, normally, in *ed*: *talked, walked, displayed.* However, there are irregular verbs that have other endings: *bought, written, sung, etc.*

The present participle is used to contruct continous tenses: *she **was teaching**, she **is teaching**, she **will be teaching**.* It sometimes works as a noun (it can then be called a gerund): *learning is good.*

The past participle follows an auxilliary verb to form the perfect past tense: *I **have taught**, they **have learned***. The passive voice uses an auxilliary with a past participle: *the class **was cheated out** of their expected success, the in-service day **was cancelled***.

Both participles can be used as adjectives: *broken, breaking, entangled*.

Phoneme A single speech sound. We use 44–48 different phonemes when we speak, depending on the accent we use. Spelling tries to represent phonemes but tries to do other things as well that may conflict with that attempt. The letters *th* in *this* represent one phoneme but in *thing* they represent a different phoneme.

Phonetics Phonetics is a way of describing the sounds we use in speech. It has nothing to do with phonics.

Phrase A group of words without a verb (it would be a clause if it had a finite verb). Phrases can be **nouns**: *the twentieth position in the class*; **adjectives**: *very clever*; **adverbs**: *too early*; or **verbs**: *was practising*.

Plural The plural form of a noun shows that more than one thing is being referred to. Plural nouns typically end in *s* (*book + s = books; girl + s = girls*), *es* (*box + es = boxes, circus + es = circuses*) or *ies* (*fairy* becomes *fairies*, *story* becomes *stories*). There are also some irregular plurals, such as *children, women, men, geese, sheep*.

Possessive Possessive pronouns – *my/mine*, etc – show who or what owns what: *my whiteboard, its cursor*. In writing, nouns show possession by adding an apostrophe and, as appropriate, the letter *s*.

Predicate The part of a sentence that is not the subject; it is about the subject: *The headteacher **arrived too early***.

Prefix A **morpheme** that is added at the beginning of a word: *a* in *atheist, un* in *unhelpful*.

Preposition Prepositions usually link a noun or noun phrase with another one or with a verb. Prepositions such as *at, on, in, over, by, with, near, through* are used to introduce adjective phrases in *The display **over** the radiator* or *That boy **by** the boundary fence* and to introduce adverb phrases in *Joe is **on** the go as usual* and *Annie's balloon rose **into** the sky*.

Pronoun A word used instead of a noun, a noun phrase or a group of nouns. It may be a **personal pronoun**: *I/me, you/you, he/him, she/her, it/it, we/us, they/them*; a **possessive pronoun**: *my/mine, your/yours, his/his, her/hers, our/ours, their/theirs, its/its*; a **reflexive pronoun**: *myself, herself, themselves*; or an **interrogative pronoun** (used in questions): *who/whom, whose, which, what*.

Punctuation The standard set of marks used in written and printed texts to clarify meaning and to separate sentences, words and parts of words. The most commonly used punctuation marks in English are:
- **apostrophe** (')
- **colon** (:)
- **comma** (,)
- **exclamation mark** (!)
- **full stop** (.)
- **hyphen** (-)
- **inverted commas** (see *speech marks*)
- **parentheses** (singular: *parenthesis*, also known as brackets or ellipses (singular, ellipsis) (( ))
- **semi-colon** (;)

- **speech marks**, also known as quotation marks or inverted commas (" " or ' '), and
- **question mark** (?).

Also included are special signals such as:

- the use of a space before and after a block or words to indicate the start of a new **paragraph**, and
- the convention of using an upper case (or capital) letter to begin a proper name or a new sentence.

*Redundancy Redundancy is the use of duplicative, unnecessary or useless wording, also known as **tautology**.

Relative clause Relative clauses come after nouns and function as adjectives. Typically, they open with a relative pronoun: *who, whom, that, which, whose: The teacher **that we hoped to appoint** was not as experienced as two other candidates.* Note that, in this case, the relative pronoun, *that,* can be deleted without losing the meaning.

Sentence A sentence is a clause or a group of clauses. Each clause needs to have a finite verb.

- **Finite verbs** are ones that tell us about tense; they almost invariably have a subject: *Ann and Tony both found maths easy.*
- **Non-finite verb** forms are the infinitive – *to teach* – and the participles that end in *–ed* or *–ing*.
- Sentences can be **declarative**: *The class rushed into the hall*; **interrogative**: *Can't your class do anything quietly?*; **imperative**: *Slow Down!* or **exclamative**: *That's great!*

*Sentence stem In the test items, this is the first part of a sentence that requires completion by choosing from several possible endings, for example:

There were four kinds of meetings that day: … followed by a list.

Singular Nouns can be singular or plural: *book* or *books*; *woman* or *women*. Verbs can also show singularity – *I teach, she teaches* – or plurality – *we teach, they teach.*

*Standard English The variety of English used in public communication, particularly in writing.

*Statement A sentence that contains a fact or proposition, for example, *this is a glossary.*

Subject A sentence has a subject (a noun or a pronoun) that does something (the verb): ***She*** *taught sentence-structure very clearly.*

Suffix A **morpheme** that is added at the end of a word: *ed* in *walked, ful* in *helpful.*

Syntax Grammar: how sentences are organised.

Tautology The unnecessary repetition of the same idea in different words: in *The Governors met together,* the last word is unnecessary.

*Unit of meaning An identifiably discrete idea.

Verb Words that say what we do or are: *The teacher **stopped** the class because one child **was being** silly.*

- **Active verbs** (verbs in the active voice) tell us what someone did: *Lucy **thanked** the teacher.* **Passive verbs** (verbs in the passive voice) tell us what was done to somebody: *The teacher was **thanked** by Lucy.*
- **Auxilliary verbs** – the main ones are *be, have, do* – accompany main verbs to show tense: *They **have** painted, they **do** run.* Some, called **modal verbs**, express

possibility or obligation: *can, could, may, might, will, would, shall, should, must, ought to.*

- **Tense** is the way that a verb tells us when something happened. This is shown in the different forms of the verb, from the past – *learned, has learned, had learned* – to the present – *learns, is learning, does learn* – to the future – *will learn, will have learned*, etc.
- **Number** is the way that a verb shows if one or more than one **subject** did something: *Alice sings, Annie and Joe sing.*

*Vowel The letters a, e, i, o, u; see also **consonant**.

Note

Entries marked with * have been reproduced by courtesy of the TDA © Training and Development Agency for Schools. Permission to reproduce TDA copyright material does not extend to any material that is identifed as being the copyright of a third party nor to any photographs.